PLI's Guide
to the
Sarbanes-Oxley Act
for Business Professionals

Practising Law Institute's
Corporate and Securities Law Library

Series Editor

Larry D. Soderquist
Professor, Vanderbilt University Law School
Of Counsel, Baker, Donelson, Bearman, Caldwell & Berkowitz, PC
Nashville, Tennessee

PLI course handbooks on securities law topics are also available. Please ask for a catalog.

Practising Law Institute
810 Seventh Avenue
New York, New York 10019
(800) 260-4754
fax: (800) 321-0093
www.pli.edu

PLI's Guide
to the
Sarbanes-Oxley Act
for Business Professionals

Directors • Officers • Accountants
Financial Advisors • Lawyers

John T. Bostelman

Sullivan & Cromwell LLP

Practising Law Institute
New York City

Order #4905

This work is designed to provide practical and useful information on the subject matter covered. However, it is sold with the understanding that neither the publisher nor the author is engaged in rendering legal, accounting or other professional services. If legal advice or other expert assistance is required, the services of a competent professional should be sought.

QUESTIONS ABOUT THIS BOOK?

If you have questions about replacement pages, billing or shipments, or would like information on our other products, please contact our **customer service department** at (800) 260-4PLI.

For library-related queries, **law librarians** may call toll-free (877) 900-5291 or email: libraryrelations@pli.edu.

For any other questions or suggestions about this book, contact PLI's **editorial department** at: editorial@pli.edu.

For general information about Practising Law Institute, please visit **www.pli.edu**.

Library of Congress Control Number: 2004117314

ISBN: 1-4024-0480-8

For my wife, Emily Hannah—
whose encouragement and support were essential.

About the Author

JOHN T. BOSTELMAN is a partner of Sullivan & Cromwell LLP and brings to this book twenty-five years of experience in securities law, corporate advice, and governance matters. He is the author of *The Sarbanes-Oxley Deskbook* (Practising Law Institute, 2003), a 2,000-page legal treatise called the "bible for securities lawyers" by *Fortune Magazine*.

Mr. Bostelman coordinates his firm's securities practice from its New York office and has been a speaker for numerous organizations, including the Practising Law Institute and conferences of the American Bar Association. He serves as Chair of the Securities Registration Subcommittee of the ABA Committee on Federal Regulation of Securities. He graduated from Yale University (B.A., 1975) and Columbia University Law School (J.D., 1979).

Sullivan & Cromwell LLP is a pre-eminent international law firm conducting a global practice through a network of offices that links many of the world's leading political and financial centers, with 700 lawyers in twelve offices worldwide. From its earliest involvement in the formation of Edison General Electric Company in 1882 and United States Steel Corporation in 1901 to its present work with the companies that are leading the global economy into the twenty-first century, the firm has been closely involved in the affairs of some of America's greatest industrial, commercial and financial enterprises.

Acknowledgement

The author acknowledges with thanks the assistance of Xiaodong Yi, his colleague at Sullivan & Cromwell LLP, in the writing of this book.

Table of Chapters

Table of Compliance Checklists

Table of Contents

Chapter 5   Disclosure of Non-GAAP Financial Measures

Chapter 9   Other Director Governance Matters .. 101

Chapter 12 Public Company Accounting Oversight Board 137

Chapter 1

Introduction

Purpose of This Book

The effects of the Sarbanes-Oxley Act (SOA) and related reforms now permeate U.S. corporate and financial life and have been exported to non-U.S. companies whose securities are listed in the United States. The purpose of this book is to describe all the new requirements in terms that are useful for business professionals and others who do not need to become experts but want to understand better the myriad new rules and regulations.

This book avoids use of legal jargon and technical references but still seeks to explain the new requirements sufficiently to be a serious business reference tool. Supplementing the explanations are subject-oriented checklists that pull the material together from different perspectives, such as the responsibilities of an audit committee or the use

1

of non-GAAP financial measures in reporting financial results. At the end of each chapter are references to the related SEC or other rules and to the official SEC website commentary, to aid in any desired follow-up with professional advisors.

It is possible to organize the provisions of the Sarbanes-Oxley Act and related stock exchange corporate governance reforms into several broad categories, each corresponding to a part of this book:

- public disclosure of financial information and regulation of insider conflicts (**chapters 2–6**);

- corporate governance matters, such as the structure and duties of the board of directors, the audit committee and other committees (**chapters 7–10**);

- regulation of auditors (**chapters 11 and 12**);

- new rules for attorneys (**chapter 13**);

- responsibilities of ancillary gatekeepers, such as research analysts (**chapters 14 and 15**);

- record keeping (**chapter 16**); and

- remedies and penalties (**chapter 17**).

The information in this book is current as of October 31, 2004.

Scope of the Sarbanes-Oxley Act

Most of the provisions of the Sarbanes-Oxley Act apply only to an "issuer," as defined in the SOA. Thus, the SOA's scope is generally defined by status as an "issuer" or a specified relationship to an "issuer," such as officer, director, auditor or attorney to an issuer.

A few provisions of the SOA, such as part of the employee whistleblower protection discussed in chapter 14 and the record keeping requirements discussed in chapter 16, apply to any person, regardless of the person's or entity's status as an "issuer" or as having a specified relationship with an "issuer."

Entities That Are Issuers

The definition of "issuer" in the SOA encompasses all types of registrants that file disclosure documents with the SEC, including all public companies in the United States and all non-U.S. companies having securities listed on a U.S. exchange or traded in Nasdaq (for example, Level II or III ADR programs). "Issuer" also includes a company that has a pending registration statement with the SEC for an initial public offering of equity or debt.

The definition of issuer includes virtually all SEC-registered mutual funds and SEC-registered closed-end investment companies. The definition also includes unit investment trusts and asset-backed issuers at least during their first fiscal year and, if they have listed securities, thereafter. The SEC rules in some cases apply differently for registered investment companies or asset-backed issuers than for industrial companies.

In this book, the term "public company" is used to refer to "issuers" to which the SOA applies as described above.

Entities That Are Not Issuers

The definition of "issuer" does not extend to non-U.S. companies that have perfected an exemption from registration pursuant to Exchange Act Rule 12g3-2(b) (including Level I ADR programs), even though their securities may be publicly traded or listed outside the United States.

A non-U.S. government or governmental entity eligible to use Securities Act Schedule B to register securities offerings with the SEC would also not be within the definition of "issuer" unless its securities are listed on the NYSE or another U.S. securities exchange.

Philosophy of the Sarbanes-Oxley Act

The SOA does not contain a statement of legislative purpose, as did some of the Depression-era federal securities laws that are the foundation of today's securities regulation. It is clear, though, from the legislative history, that the primary goal of the SOA is to restore investor confidence by improving corporate financial reporting.

While not spelled out in the legislative history, the philosophy of the SOA to achieve its goal is also relatively clear:

- make management more accountable;
- increase required disclosure;
- strengthen the authority and obligations of corporate gatekeepers and outside advisors;
- remove conflicts of interest of management, auditors, gatekeepers and advisors;
- regulate auditors more strongly;
- strengthen the SEC; and
- improve guidance about accounting standards.

Besides imposing a rulemaking timetable for the SEC that was relatively unique in its breadth and speed and adding numerous specific new requirements, the SOA signaled a philosophical shift in SEC regulation to a much more prescriptive approach. It is likely that the SEC will remain active in promulgating rules mandating more and earlier disclosure, beyond the requirements of the SOA.

Background: Twelve Months Leading Up to the Sarbanes-Oxley Act

The twelve months from the resignation of the CEO of Enron Corp. on August 14, 2001, to the enactment of the SOA on July 30, 2002, saw the swift collapse of Enron, overlapping reform proposals by legislative, regulatory and private-sector bodies, revelations of accounting fraud or management misdeeds at several other companies, the even more spectacular WorldCom fraud and the demise of one of the Big Five accounting firms.

These events were followed by enactment of the SOA, the broadest package of federal disclosure and corporate governance legislation since the federal securities laws were first enacted in the 1930s. Most elements of the SOA can be traced directly to problems identified at

Enron, WorldCom or other companies that came to light during 2002 while legislation was pending.

Enron

Enron's Financial Collapse

On August 14, 2001, the day Enron Corp.'s second quarter Form 10-Q was filed, Jeffrey Skilling, Enron's CEO, surprised the financial community by resigning after only six months in that position, contributing to speculation about possible problems at the company.

On October 16, 2001, Enron announced its third quarter results, including a $544 million unexpected earnings charge and a subsequently disclosed $1.2 billion reduction in stockholders' equity. On October 22, Enron announced that the SEC had requested information about some of the related party transactions discussed in the earnings announcement. On October 24, Enron announced that Andrew Fastow, its CFO, would be replaced. On November 8, Enron further announced it would restate its financial statements for the first and second quarters of 2001 and the four years 1997 through 2000, reflecting an aggregate $586 million overstatement of net income.

On December 2, 2001, after a failed effort to be acquired by rival Dynegy, Inc., Enron and some of its subsidiaries filed for reorganization under Chapter 11 of the U.S. Bankruptcy Code. At the time, this was the largest company to declare bankruptcy in U.S. history.

Some Identified Issues at Enron

An important factor that contributed to Enron's decline and eventual collapse was its series of off-balance-sheet transactions with various special purpose entities controlled by Andrew Fastow, its CFO, or by other Enron employees. Through some of these highly complex transactions, Enron sought to achieve favorable financial statement results by keeping assets and liabilities off its balance sheet, rather than to accomplish *bona fide* economic objectives or to transfer risk. In other transactions, Enron employed sophisticated structures, often funded with Enron stock or contingent stock-delivery contracts, to "hedge" against declines in Enron's merchant investments, while in fact no substantive transfers of economic risk were undertaken. In so doing, Enron was reportedly able to conceal its substantial investment losses until the decline in Enron stock resulted in the shortfall in the structuring entities' credit capacity, leading to the collapse of these hedging transactions. Enron's off-balance-sheet transactions also raised many corporate governance issues, as Enron's board of directors did not appear to have carefully scrutinized the inherent conflicts of interest in these related-party transactions nor adequately exercised an oversight role regarding the company's internal controls.

In addition, it appeared that the three major credit rating agencies in the United States—Moody's Investors Service, Standard & Poor's Corporation and Fitch Ratings—failed to identify Enron's problems during the weeks and months leading to Enron's collapse. According to Congressional investigators, investment bankers working on the proposed Enron-Dynegy merger even tried to lobby credit rating agencies in order to salvage Enron's ratings so that the deal would not fall apart.

During the period following August 2001, Enron Chairman and acting CEO Kenneth Lay was also reported to have sold substantial amounts of Enron stock, including during a period when Enron employees were blacked out from selling or allocating out of the Enron stock account in their 401(k) plan while the Enron stock price quickly declined.

Arthur Andersen's Document Destruction and Indictment

On January 10, 2002, Arthur Andersen LLP, Enron's auditing firm, made the surprising disclosure to Congressional investigators that it had destroyed a significant but undetermined number of Enron-related audit documents in October 2001, around the time of the SEC's first inquiry into Enron's accounting for SPEs and related matters.

On March 14, the U.S. Justice Department announced that Arthur Andersen LLP had been criminally indicted. The indictment, reportedly the first criminal charge brought against a major accounting firm, charged Andersen with a single count of obstruction of justice based on the Enron document destruction.

On June 15, the jury in the Arthur Andersen LLP trial handed down a guilty verdict on that charge. The firm ceased operations by August 31, 2002, approximately one year after Skilling's resignation as Enron's CEO.

Other Corporate Accounting Scandals

Other corporate accounting scandals uncovered at major companies in 2002 fueled the sense that changes were needed.

Following Enron's December 2001 bankruptcy, Global Crossing Ltd., a telecommunications company invested heavily in fiber optic and other high-speed internet lines, filed for bankruptcy in January 2002. The company's filing was, until WorldCom's in June 2002, reportedly the largest bankruptcy by a telecommunications company.

On March 27, 2002, Adelphia Communications Corporation, the nation's sixth-largest cable television operator, disclosed in its 2001 fourth-quarter earnings release the existence of $2.3 billion in off-balance-sheet debt that it co-borrowed with certain entities controlled by the Rigas family, who founded and controlled Adelphia. On May 2, 2002, Adelphia announced that it expected to restate its financial results for the past three years.

Another company that received extensive coverage for its corporate misdeeds in 2002 was Tyco International Ltd. L. Dennis Kozlowski, Tyco's CEO, together with its CFO and general counsel, was engulfed in controversies regarding their receipt of millions of dollars in questionable bonuses, loans and other payments from the company; and questions were raised about whether PricewaterhouseCoopers, Tyco's auditor, knew about these payments and whether PricewaterhouseCoopers had signed off properly on related disclosure issues.

On June 25, 2002, WorldCom, Inc., the nation's second-largest long-distance carrier and the largest handler of Internet traffic, shocked the world with its disclosure that it had overstated its cash flow by more than $3.8 billion during the previous five quarters, primarily because it improperly booked operating costs as capital investments. Moving with unprecedented speed, the SEC filed fraud charges against WorldCom the next day, and the graveness of the company's revelation also prompted President Bush to vow to hold people accountable for the bookkeeping scandal. The collapse of the company was swift: WorldCom filed for bankruptcy less than one month later on July 21, 2002. With over $107 billion of assets listed in the filing, it surpassed Enron as the largest bankruptcy case in U.S. history.

In addition to the companies discussed above, controversies surrounding Qwest Communications International and Xerox in 2002 also raised serious questions about corporate governance and accounting practices.

Regulatory Responses

The December 2001 Enron collapse and corporate accounting scandals at other major companies led to major regulatory responses from all fronts in the first half of 2002. These included the SEC's rule proposals, virtually all of which were later addressed in the SOA, President Bush's ten-point plan of reforms, the New York Stock Exchange and Nasdaq's corporate governance reform proposals and numerous congressional investigations, hearings and legislative proposals.

Enactment of the Sarbanes-Oxley Act

The House passed a modest reform bill in April 2002. Spurred by the June 2002 WorldCom collapse, the Senate passed a much tougher bill in July 2002 that became the base for the SOA. In the House-Senate conference to "reconcile" the two bills, additional changes were made that toughened the proposed law even further. It was signed into law by President Bush on July 30, 2002. Because of the speed of the SOA's passage, there is only limited legislative history available to assist in interpreting the law.

Chapter 2

Management Certifications

Penalties
NYSE CEO Certification
References

Overview

The SEC requires management certification in public companies' quarterly and annual SEC reports. These rules:

- require CEOs and CFOs to certify annual reports on Form 10-K and quarterly reports on Form 10-Q of U.S. companies and annual reports on Form 20-F or 40-F of non-U.S. companies;

- apply equally to U.S. and non-U.S. public companies; and

- require disclosure in each certified report about the results of the evaluation of disclosure controls and procedures (discussed below).

SEC rules also require each public company covered by the certification rules to maintain:

- "disclosure controls and procedures," a defined term that refers to controls and procedures designed to ensure that financial and non-financial information is fully and accurately disclosed on a timely basis; and

- "internal control over financial reporting," another defined term relating to accounting and financial reporting controls.

The two terms overlap and are discussed in chapter 3.

Scope of Certification Rules

The management certification rules require a public company's principal executive officer and principal financial officer each to certify as to enumerated matters in each annual report, such as Form 10-K for U.S. companies and Form 20-F or 40-F for non-U.S. companies.

For U.S. companies, the officers must also certify each quarterly report, such as Form 10-Q. Certification is also required for amendments to these reports.

Companies Covered

The certification rules apply to "issuers," as defined in the SOA. These are U.S. and non-U.S. companies subject to the SEC's periodic reporting requirements or that have pending securities offering registration statements (for example, for an initial public offering in the United States). Issuers include U.S. public companies, whether or not their securities are listed on a stock exchange or traded on Nasdaq. Issuers also include non-U.S. companies having listed or Nasdaq-traded securities.

The SEC staff has stated that companies filing periodic reports voluntarily with the SEC, while not considered "issuers" for SOA purposes, would nevertheless be subject to the certification requirements because the certification is a part of the forms.

The certifications are also required for registered investment companies and for asset-backed issuers. Certifications do not apply to filings by non-U.S. governmental entities eligible for Securities Act Schedule B.

Filings Covered

The certification rules apply to quarterly reports on Form 10-Q and annual reports on Form 10-K of U.S. companies, annual reports on Form 20-F of non-U.S. SEC-reporting companies and annual reports on Form 40-F of SEC-reporting Canadian companies. Certification is also required for amendments to any of those reports. The certification rules do not apply to reports on Forms 8-K, 6-K or 11-K or to submissions by non-U.S. companies pursuant to Exchange Act Rule 12g3-2(b).

Form 10-K permits the disclosure requirements of Part III (Items 10–14, relating mainly to officers and directors) to be satisfied by incorporating by reference the issuer's annual meeting proxy statement to be filed in the future, as long as the proxy statement is filed within 120 days after the end of the fiscal year covered by the Form 10-K. In these circumstances the SEC has stated that the certifications included in Form 10-K would be considered to cover the Part III information in the company's proxy statement "as and when filed." Therefore, in connection with filing the proxy statement the certifying officers should conduct the same type of procedures to support their certifications *vis-à-vis* the Part III disclosures as they conducted in connection with filing the Form 10-K regarding the other 10-K disclosures, even though no new certifications are required with the proxy statement itself.

The certifications became effective for reports and amendments filed on or after August 29, 2002.

Content of Certification

The certification contains representations regarding the following matters, most of which are dictated by the SOA itself:

- review of the periodic report (certification paragraph 1);

- material accuracy of the periodic report (certification paragraph 2);

- fair presentation of financial information (certification paragraph 3);

- disclosure controls and procedures (certification paragraph 4(a) and (c)); and

- internal control over financial reporting (certification paragraphs 4(b) and (d) and 5).

The required wording of the certification is set forth in the exhibit requirements of the affected forms and may not be changed.

Paragraph 1—Review

Paragraph 1 requires the signing officer to state that he or she has reviewed the report being certified. The SEC has not clarified the meaning of "review," which tracks the SOA itself. Signing officers would be prudent to assume that the term will be interpreted to mean they are certifying they have fully read the report.

Paragraph 2—Material Accuracy

Paragraph 2 requires the signing officer to state that, based on the officer's knowledge, the report does not contain any material misstatements or any materially misleading statements. The wording of certification paragraph 2 tracks that of Exchange Act Rule 10b-5, the general antifraud rule. The same language is also used in a rule requiring that SEC periodic reports include additional information, beyond that specifically required by the forms and rules, necessary to prevent the statements in the report from being materially misleading.

The SEC has noted that certification paragraph 2 also covers executive compensation disclosure and other information incorporated by reference from annual proxy materials. The certification should be interpreted to cover these future documents "as and when filed," according to the SEC.

The SEC has also stated that the certifications in paragraphs 2 and 3 are made in the context of the requirements of the particular report being certified. In particular, the certification is not intended to require expanding the abbreviated disclosure in quarterly reports to meet the requirements of annual reports.

Paragraph 3—Fair Presentation of Financial Information

Paragraph 3 requires the signing officer to state that, based on the officer's knowledge, the financial statements and other financial information in the report "fairly present" in all material respects the financial condition, results of operations and cash flows for the periods presented.

The SEC has clarified that the covered financial disclosure includes financial statements (including footnotes), selected financial data, management's discussion and analysis and other financial information. The SEC has also emphasized that "fairly present" is not limited by reference to generally accepted accounting principles. Rather, the certifying officers should use a standard of overall material accuracy and completeness.

Finally, as noted above in the discussion of certification paragraph 2, the SEC has stated that the certifications in paragraphs 2 and 3 are made in the context of the particular report. Thus, the financial statements and related footnote disclosure of a Form 10-Q may continue to be presented in condensed form, as permitted by SEC rules, and need not be expanded to the scope of full annual financial statements.

Paragraphs 4(a) and 4(c)—Evaluation of Disclosure Controls and Procedures

Paragraph 4 requires the signing officer to state that he or she and the other certifying officer(s) are responsible for "disclosure controls and procedures" and "internal control over financial reporting." Additional statements about disclosure controls and procedures are covered in paragraphs 4(a) and 4(c):

- Paragraph 4(a)—the certifying officer has designed them or supervised their design to ensure that material information is made known to the officer by others within the company and its consolidated subsidiaries; and

- Paragraph 4(c)—the officer has presented elsewhere in the report the officer's conclusions about the effectiveness of the procedures based on an evaluation as of the end of the quarter or year covered by the report.

The term "disclosure controls and procedures" is defined under SEC rules as controls and other procedures of a public company that are designed to ensure that both non-financial and financial information required to be disclosed by the company in its periodic reports is recorded, processed, summarized and reported in a timely fashion. The rules require all public companies to have disclosure controls and procedures, as described in more detail in chapter 3.

The evaluation on which disclosure is based must be made for the period covered by the report. For U.S. public companies, the evaluation must be made for each fiscal quarter, including the fourth quarter (that is, the year-end evaluation should include both the evaluation required in connection with management's internal control report described in chapter 3 and an evaluation for the fourth quarter). For non-U.S. public companies that file with the SEC, the evaluation must be made annually.

The SEC expects each public company to develop a process for reviewing and evaluating its disclosure controls and procedures according to its particular business and internal management and supervisory practices. The SEC recommends that issuers create a committee responsible for disclosure matters that would report to senior management.

Paragraphs 4(b), 4(d) and 5—Internal Control Over Financial Reporting

As noted above, paragraph 4 requires the signing officer to state that he or she and the other certifying officers are responsible for "disclosure controls and procedures" (discussed above) and "internal control over financial reporting." Additional statements about internal control over financial reporting are covered in paragraphs 4(b), 4(d) and 5.

Meaning of "Internal Control Over Financial Reporting"

The reference to "internal control over financial reporting" in certification paragraphs 4(b), 4(d) and 5 has a meaning different from "disclosure controls and procedures," discussed above. "Internal control over financial reporting" refers to accounting and financial reporting controls and includes three elements:

- the maintenance of records that accurately, fairly and in reasonable detail reflect transactions and dispositions of assets;

- reasonable assurance that transactions are recorded so as to permit preparation of financial statements in accordance with generally accepted accounting principles and that receipts and expenditures are made only in accordance with management authorization; and

- reasonable assurance regarding prevention or detection of unauthorized acquisition, use or disposition of the company's assets.

The SEC has provided little guidance on the extent of the overlap between the concepts of "internal control over financial reporting" and "disclosure controls and procedures."

Paragraphs 4(b) and 4(d)

CEOs and CFOs must certify in paragraphs 4(b) and 4(d) of their certifications that:

- Paragraph 4(b)—the certifying officer has designed or supervised the design of internal control over financial reporting to provide reasonable assurance regarding reliability of financial reporting and preparation of financial statements in accordance with generally accepted accounting principles; and

- Paragraph 4(d)—the officer has disclosed in the report any change in internal control over financial reporting that occurred during the most recent fiscal quarter (or fiscal year in the case of a non-U.S. SEC-reporting company) that has materially affected, or is reasonably likely to materially affect, the company's internal control over financial reporting.

Until a company is required to comply with the internal control audit requirement described in chapter 3, the company's certifying officers may temporarily modify the content of their certifications to eliminate paragraph 4(b) and the reference to internal control over financial reporting in the introductory language in paragraph 4 that refers to the certifying officers' responsibility for establishing and maintaining internal control over financial reporting for the company. They may not omit paragraphs 4(d) and 5.

Paragraph 5

Paragraph 5 requires the certifying officer to state that he or she has disclosed to the company's auditors and audit committee:

- all "significant deficiencies" and "material weaknesses" in internal control over financial reporting that are reasonably likely to adversely affect the company's ability to record, process, summarize and report financial information; and

- any fraud, whether or not material, that involves management or other employees who have a significant role in internal control over financial reporting.

The rule does not define "significant deficiencies" or "material weaknesses." However, the SEC has stated that these terms have the same meanings as under generally accepted auditing standards and attestation standards. Under those standards, a "material weakness," the most serious level of concern, is a subset of "significant deficiency." The Public Company Accounting Oversight Board has adopted an auditing standard that defines these terms somewhat more stringently than the previous auditing standard. The SEC has confirmed that those definitions also apply to management certifications. These terms are discussed in chapter 3.

The SEC has not specified the exact point at which management must evaluate the controls to detect significant deficiencies, material weaknesses or fraud and refers only to the certifying officers' "most recent evaluation." This contrasts with the certification relating to disclosure controls and procedures, which requires the evaluation to be as of the end of the period covered by a report. In the absence of guidance, it would appear reasonable for the evaluation of internal control over financial reporting to occur in any manner considered reasonable by management. Management's analysis to support the annual internal control report described in chapter 3 should be sufficient to address the annual evaluation requirement for certification paragraphs 4(b), 4(d) and 5. Presumably quarterly evaluations by U.S. companies may be more limited.

The SEC rule does not define what is meant by "fraud," "involves" or "management" in the paragraph 5 certification, and the SEC has not provided further guidance. Based on other securities law uses of the term, it would be reasonable to assume that "fraud" requires a degree of scienter on the part of the primary actor (for example, reckless or intentional conduct) and that "management" encompasses executive officers (and perhaps directors). It is unclear whether "involves" would encompass aiding and abetting or failure to supervise (through negligence or otherwise). In the absence of further guidance, CEOs and CFOs may decide to err on the side of over-reporting to the auditors and audit committee.

Disclosure About Evaluation and Changes

The SEC rules require disclosure in the report being certified about the evaluation of the disclosure controls and procedures and disclosure of any material changes in internal control over financial reporting. These required disclosures are referred to in certification paragraphs 4(c) and 4(d).

Certification Paragraph 4(c) Disclosure About Evaluation of Disclosure Controls

The report must contain a statement whether, based on their evaluation, the CEO and CFO concluded that the company's disclosure controls and procedures were effective. Unlike the certification itself, from which no deviation in wording is permitted, the form of disclosure about the effectiveness evaluation is not prescribed. Actual disclosures have varied. Variations have included adding a qualification that the procedures were "effective in all material respects," adding a disclaimer about the inherent limitations of disclosure controls and softening the conclusion from "were effective" to "provided reasonable assurance of effectiveness" or to "were effective in timely alerting officers to material information required to be included in reports."

There is no requirement to disclose *changes* in disclosure controls and procedures made between evaluations or between report dates—only their effectiveness. For internal control over financial reporting, material changes must be publicly disclosed in the report, as discussed below, and material weaknesses must be disclosed annually, as discussed in chapter 3.

Certification Paragraph 4(d) Disclosure About Changes to Internal Control Over Financial Reporting

The SEC rules require disclosure in the report of changes that are reasonably likely materially to affect internal control over financial reporting. Disclosure is required only when there have been material changes during the period covered by the report, although some companies have chosen also to disclose that there have been no changes. Of course, if material changes have occurred, they must be described.

The SEC has cautioned that, although the rules do not explicitly require a company to disclose the reasons for any change to its internal control over financial reporting that occurred during a report period or to otherwise elaborate about the change, the company will have to determine, on a facts and circumstances basis, whether the reasons for the change, or other information about the circumstances surrounding the change, must be included to prevent the disclosure about the change from being materially misleading.

Mechanics of Certification

Form

The SEC has stated that the certification must be in exactly the form specified by the SEC rules, and the wording of the certification may not be changed in any respect even if the change appears inconsequential in nature, except that "other certifying officers" in certification paragraph 4 may be changed to the singular if there are only two certifying officers in total. The rules also provide that persons required to provide the certification must do so personally and may not have the certification signed on their behalf pursuant to a power of attorney.

As previously noted, until the audit of internal control described in chapter 3 is required, a company's certifying officers may temporarily modify the content of their certifications to eliminate paragraph 4(b) and the reference to internal control over financial reporting in the introductory language in paragraph 4 that refers to the certifying officers' responsibility for establishing and maintaining internal control over financial reporting for the company.

Signatures

The CEO and CFO must sign separate, but identical, certifications. The individual's title should be placed under the signature to indicate whether he or she is signing as principal executive officer or principal financial officer. If the same individual performs both functions, a single certification may be furnished listing both titles under the signature.

The officer holding the relevant position at the time of filing must sign. A new CEO or CFO who joined after quarter-end but before filing must sign. Where a CEO or CFO is planning to resign but is still employed, and an interim CEO or CFO is performing those functions at the time of filing, the interim officer must sign. Where an issuer does not have a CEO or CFO, the person performing the function must sign. Co-CEOs or Co-CFOs should each sign separate certifications.

Location and Submission

The certifications must be filed as exhibits to the report. There is no requirement for notarization.

Certification Required by Section 906 of the Sarbanes-Oxley Act

The SOA also includes a second management certification requirement. This second requirement is largely redundant to the SEC certification described earlier in this chapter. Its inclusion is probably a congressional oversight, but it remains a requirement.

This second certification is required by SOA section 906, which added a provision to the Federal Criminal Code requiring that chief executive officers and chief financial officers of public companies certify annual and quarterly SEC reports. The certification required by SOA section 906 is separate from that required by the SEC described previously in this chapter.

The section 906 certification is within the jurisdiction of the U.S. Department of Justice, not the SEC, and there are no clarifying rules. Violations are punishable only if they rise to the level of criminal offenses. For this reason, the section 906 certification is sometimes referred to as the "criminal certification."

Reports Covered

The SOA section 906 certification is required to accompany quarterly reports on Form 10-Q and annual reports on Form 10-K for U.S. public companies, annual reports on Form 20-F for non-U.S. SEC-reporting companies and annual reports on Form 40-F for Canadian

SEC-reporting companies that use that form. The section 906 certification became effective for reports and amendments filed on or after July 30, 2002.

The section 906 certification is not required to accompany Form 8-K reports of U.S. public companies, Form 6-K reports of non-U.S. public companies or Form 11-K reports of benefit plans.

Content of Certification

Neither the SEC nor the U.S. Department of Justice has promulgated any form of section 906 certification. The SOA itself states that the certification must state two things—that the report "fully complies" with the relevant SEC requirements and that information in the report "fairly presents, in all material respects, the financial condition and results of operations" of the company. The work undertaken by CEOs and CFOs to support the SEC management certifications described previously in this chapter is generally considered sufficient to support the section 906 certification.

Although the SEC rules state that both officers are permitted to sign a single section 906 certification (in contrast to the SEC management certifications, which must be separate), it would still be advisable that separate section 906 certifications be completed by the CEO and CFO.

It should be permissible for the certifying officers to state that the certification is made "to my knowledge." Companies should balance the possible public relations risk that the inclusion of a knowledge qualification may cause them to be unfavorably compared with other companies that do not include such a qualification against the potential disclosure liability concern that exists from not pointing out that the certification is inherently not absolute.

The "fully complies" certification is not qualified by materiality. Presumably, as a matter of prosecutorial discretion, the U.S. Department of Justice, the agency generally responsible for prosecution under the Federal Criminal Code, would not seek to prosecute a CEO or CFO for immaterial non-compliance, particularly where a good-faith effort to assure full compliance had been made and a good-faith belief about full compliance existed. One could reasonably use the process supporting the SEC certifications previously discussed in this chapter also to satisfy the section 906 "fully complies" certification. This process should include not only a "form check," but also efforts to ensure the report satisfy the SEC requirement that it contain no material misstatements or materially misleading statements.

The "fairly presents" certification, while qualified by materiality, covers all information in the report, not only financial information. Like paragraph 3 of the SEC certifications, it is not qualified by generally accepted accounting principles. Yet the meaning of "fairly presents" is not clear outside the sense used in generally accepted accounting principles to describe financial statements. Nevertheless, it is difficult to imagine a situation where satisfaction of paragraphs 2 (the general disclosure certification) and 3 (the financial statements fairly present certification) of the SEC certifications should not also satisfy the "fairly presents" certification of section 906.

Submission Method

SEC rules require that SOA section 906 certifications be submitted as exhibits to the related periodic reports. Fortunately, these certifications are not automatically incorporated by reference into securities offerings registration statements.

Penalties

Persons knowingly making defective section 906 certifications are subject to fines up to $1 million and imprisonment up to ten years. Persons doing so willfully and knowingly are subject to fines up to $5 million and imprisonment up to twenty years. The difference between the two states of mind (knowingly versus willfully and knowingly) is subtle, unclear in practice and defined differently by various federal courts. A willful and knowing violation is sometimes said to require not only intent to commit the act in question but also intent specifically to violate the law. In any event, the difference between the two states of mind should not be particularly important for purposes of planning conduct.

A person willfully failing to provide the section 906 certification could also be prosecuted, subject to fines up to $5 million and imprisonment up to twenty years.

Of course, willful violation of any SEC statute or rule, including the SEC certification described earlier in this chapter, also subjects the violator to similar criminal penalties—fines up to $5 million and imprisonment up to twenty years. The attention paid to the criminal penalties for violating the section 906 certification may be due to the fact that the meaning of the required certifications is not clear, as described above.

NYSE CEO Certification

The NYSE requires an annual CEO certification that a listed company is in compliance with the NYSE corporate governance listing standards. This certification is discussed in chapter 9 on page 106.

References

Sarbanes-Oxley Act
§§ 302 & 906

SEC Rules
Rules 13a-14 & 15d-14

Reg. S-K Items 307, 308 & 601(b)(31)

SEC Website (rules and commentary)
www.sec.gov/rules/final/33-8124.htm
(August 2002 initial rules)

www.sec.gov/rules/final/33-8238.htm
(June 2003 amended rules)

Chapter 3

Disclosure Procedures and Financial Controls

Overview

The SEC adopted rules in conjunction with its CEO/CFO certification rules, described in chapter 2, that require each public company to maintain and evaluate "disclosure controls and procedures," a term that refers to controls and procedures designed to ensure that financial and non-financial information is fully and accurately disclosed on a timely basis.

The SEC also adopted rules mandating that companies maintain and evaluate "internal control over financial reporting." This term refers to a process designed to provide reasonable assurance regarding

25

the reliability of financial reporting and the preparation of financial statements for external purposes in accordance with generally accepted accounting principles. Companies are also required to file with each annual report an audit report on internal control by the independent auditors, commencing in 2004 for larger U.S. public companies and 2005 for other public companies.

Disclosure Procedures

The objective of the SEC's disclosure controls and procedures rules is to ensure the accuracy and timeliness of a company's SEC periodic reports. For U.S. public companies these are Forms 10-K, 10-Q and 8-K and proxy statements. For non-U.S. public companies these are Forms 20-F and 6-K (or, for some Canadian companies, Forms 40-F and 6-K).

Description of Required Procedures

SEC rules require each public company to maintain disclosure controls and procedures designed to ensure that information required to be disclosed in its SEC periodic reports is recorded, processed, summarized and reported in a timely manner. These procedures must be designed to ensure that required disclosure is communicated to the company's management, including the CEO and CFO, so that timely disclosure decisions may be made. The term "disclosure controls and procedures" is a broad concept designed to support compliance with disclosure requirements generally and is different from a company's "internal control over financial reporting," discussed later in this chapter. The SEC has stated that the procedures should cover any information required to be disclosed in a report, such as developments and risks pertaining to the company's business.

Disclosure controls and procedures must be designed, maintained and evaluated to ensure full and timely disclosure in *all periodic* reports filed or submitted to the SEC, including current reports on Form 8-K and proxy materials and, for non-U.S. public companies, reports on Form 6-K. The required scope of disclosure controls and procedures is thus broader than the CEO/CFO certification requirement described in chapter 2, which applies only to annual reports and, for U.S. public companies, quarterly reports. The SEC has stated that a company that fails to maintain the required controls and procedures could be subject to SEC enforcement action even if the failure does not result in flawed disclosure.

Management Evaluation and Related Disclosure

The SEC rules also require management to conduct an evaluation of a company's disclosure controls and procedures as of the end of the period covered by each certified report. Management, including the CEO and CFO, must undertake this evaluation. Furthermore, the CEO and CFO must certify in the report that they evaluated the effectiveness of the procedures and must present in the report their conclusions about the effectiveness of the procedures based on the required evaluation.

It is recommended that companies conduct a preliminary evaluation early enough in the reporting cycle, before the actual evaluation is conducted at the end of the report period, so that desired changes can be implemented prior to the actual evaluation. Under the SEC rules, changes to disclosure controls and procedures need not be disclosed.

If companies have chosen to have a disclosure committee, the disclosure committee would be an appropriate body to conduct the required evaluation. If companies have not chosen to have a disclosure committee, then those persons primarily responsible for disclosure matters might conduct the evaluation.

Whether or not the CEO and CFO are members of the disclosure committee, companies should consider having them participate in the most important activities of the disclosure committee, particularly the meetings with key people in the disclosure process. If they do not participate in all activities, they should review a report of the evaluation and direct any necessary follow-up. Their review should not be cursory or done so late that follow-up would be impractical.

The required disclosure about the results of the evaluation is discussed in chapter 2, in the section "Certification Paragraph 4(c) Disclosure About Evaluation of Disclosure Controls," on page 18.

Suggested Approach to Develop Procedures

To the extent that companies already had appropriate procedures before the SOA to support their disclosures in Exchange Act filings, the SEC rules do not require companies to do anything they were not already supposed to be doing. The rules, however, put pressure on companies to re-examine their procedures and enhance them where appropriate.

Based on the purpose of the procedures, it is reasonable to conclude that companies' disclosure controls and procedures should have the following attributes:

- Top management should be involved in supervising the design and operation of the procedures.

- The procedures should be written.

- They should be sufficiently detailed to lay out the overall approach and provide guidance, but sufficiently brief that they will provide flexibility for variation, will be understandable by those who need to follow them and will be followed. Where appropriate, more detailed procedures may be applicable to some groups of employees.

- They should be customized for the company's management structure, industry and business processes.

- They should be overseen by a central person or group.

- They should be reviewed and evaluated for effectiveness in a formal session conducted by top management on a quarterly basis for U.S. companies and an annual basis for non-U.S. companies.

To meet these goals, it is suggested that companies consider the following procedures.

Document Current Procedures

Companies should document in writing the current procedures used in preparing their SEC reports and proxy statements. Companies should review their current procedures and consider whether enhancements are appropriate. Management should report the results of this review to the audit committee or board of directors.

Information-Gathering Procedures

Companies should consider whether they should offer sessions, tailored for specific departments, designed to increase sensitivity to disclosure requirements. Companies should also consider whether other ways of training employees regarding disclosure requirements might be more appropriate, such as distributing written guidelines.

Companies should consider the best ways to gather information. Options include meetings, preparation of written reports and individual review and comment on a draft report. Companies should consider the efficiencies of including disclosure review at periodic management or budget meetings. Companies should consider how to ensure that the information gathered is consistent with that published elsewhere, including in public investor relations newsletters, press releases and website postings.

Companies should consider whether the appropriate business units are participating in disclosure.

Top management, including the CEO and CFO, must be personally involved in the disclosure process. This involvement requires CEO and CFO review of all reports requiring their certification. It may also include the CEO, the CFO or other members of management reviewing specific issues addressed in the report, talking with key people who prepared the report and reviewing reports with appropriate third parties.

Companies should consider whether regular review sessions should be convened in which top management can ask the key people preparing the reports whether they are comfortable with the disclosure or if they think any element of the disclosure is questionable. Management may then review the results with the audit committee and independent auditors.

Oversight/Disclosure Management

Companies should consider developing a disclosure compliance calendar in which key disclosure dates and milestones are marked.

Companies should consider whether to create an internal employee group, referred to as a "disclosure committee," with responsibility for considering the materiality of information and determining disclosure obligations on a timely basis. The SEC recommends that a company have such a committee.

Verification

Companies may wish to consider obtaining appropriate "backup" support, which may include certifications from certain officers that support those of the CEO and CFO. Back-up certification may be useful for some companies but not appropriate for others.

For those companies considering back-up certifications, it is probably most appropriate that the form of certification by lower-level or divisional employees not be expressed in terms of legal language as to "materiality," but rather should be to the effect that the employees have disclosed to more senior officers matters that have affected, or may affect, the business in ways that may be of interest or concern to senior management.

Companies should consider whether to incorporate third-party support—for example, from their independent auditors or outside counsel—into their disclosure controls and procedures. In making this determination, companies should consider whether the third-party support would provide sufficient improvements to the disclosure to justify the additional cost and time.

If outside counsel has been sufficiently involved in the company's previous disclosure process, such as through participation in due diligence for recent securities offerings or involvement in the company's periodic disclosure review process, companies could consider seeking review by outside counsel of the draft report. The extent of this review could range from seeking informal comments on all or part of the draft report and a "form check" to more formal advice on all or part of the report. Where outside counsel does not have significant current information about the matters discussed in the report, there appears to be relatively little incremental value in having only a "form check" performed by outside counsel versus relying on the efforts of inside counsel.

Companies should consider whether any areas of disclosure merit the establishment of a task force focused on those disclosures.

Coordination with Internal Financial Controls and Financial Reporting

Companies should consider how to coordinate their financial accounting and reporting process with their disclosure controls and procedures. The SEC has stated that the concept of disclosure controls and procedures is broader than that of internal accounting controls, although the SEC has provided little guidance about the extent of the overlap.

Financial Controls

The concept of internal controls in relation to accounting or financial reporting has existed for some time. The U.S. securities laws have since 1977 required public companies to maintain these controls. The SOA elaborated on what is required and mandated the independent auditors to issue an audit report on these controls in conjunction with the annual audit of the financial statements.

Internal Control Over Financial Reporting

In response to the requirements of the SOA, the SEC adopted the term "internal control over financial reporting," which is a process designed "to provide reasonable assurance regarding the reliability of financial reporting and the preparation of financial statements for external purposes in accordance with generally accepted accounting principles." This process must be designed by or under the supervision of the company's principal executive and principal financial officers and must be effected by the company's board of directors, management and other personnel. The process must address three elements:

- the maintenance of records that accurately, fairly and in reasonable detail reflect transactions and dispositions of assets;

- reasonable assurance that transactions are recorded so as to permit preparation of financial statements in accordance with generally accepted accounting principles and that receipts and expenditures are made only in accordance with management authorization; and

- reasonable assurance regarding prevention or detection of unauthorized acquisition, use or disposition of the company's assets.

The definition does not focus on other elements of internal control that relate to effectiveness and efficiency of a company's operations or a company's compliance with applicable laws and regulations, with the exception of compliance with the applicable laws and regulations directly related to the preparation of financial statements, such as the SEC's financial reporting requirements.

Annual Internal Control Reports

A public company is required to include an internal control report of management in its annual report on Form 10-K, 20-F or 40-F, beginning with the annual report for its first fiscal year ending on or after November 15, 2004, in the case of larger U.S. companies. The requirement first applies to other U.S public companies and to non-U.S. public companies beginning with the annual report for the fiscal year ending on or after July 15, 2005. Significantly, there must also be included an audit report on internal control by the independent auditors.

Management's Report on Internal Control

Management's report must state management's responsibilities for establishing and maintaining adequate "internal control over financial reporting." The CEO and CFO must participate. The SEC rules do not specify the procedures management must follow in conducting its annual evaluation. Instead, the procedures should vary depending on the company's individual circumstances. The SEC has cautioned that "inquiry alone will not provide an adequate basis for management's assessment" and that management's procedures should require both (1) evaluation of the design of internal control over financial reporting and (2) testing of its effectiveness.

Management's report must also contain a statement identifying the framework used to evaluate the effectiveness of internal control over financial reporting. Under the SEC rules, management's evaluation is required to be based on "a suitable, recognized control framework" that has been "established by a body or group that has followed due-process procedures, including the broad distribution of the framework for public comment." The SEC has stated that the framework published in a 1992 report by an organization called the Committee of Sponsoring Organizations of the Treadway Commission (COSO) meets these criteria.

Finally, management's annual report must describe conclusions about the effectiveness of the company's internal control over financial reporting based on management's evaluation of those controls as of the end of the company's most recent fiscal year. However, the evaluation (that is, the actual evaluation of the design and testing) is not required to take place at any particular time. Management is required to disclose in its report any "material weakness" (discussed in the section "Material Weakness and Significant Deficiency" below) in internal control over financial reporting and cannot conclude that internal control over financial reporting is effective if there is any material weakness.

Audit Report on Internal Control

The independent auditors that audit the financial statements included in the company's annual report must also audit internal control over financial reporting.

This new type of audit is governed by standards established by the Public Company Accounting Oversight Board (PCAOB), the regulatory body established by the SOA to oversee the auditing profession and establish auditing standards in the United States. By requiring auditors to evaluate directly the effectiveness of internal control over financial reporting, the PCAOB standard will likely increase the scope (and cost) of annual audits, heighten standards for "effective" internal control over financial reporting and enhance the obligations of management and audit committees with respect to internal control over financial reporting. The required design and documentation effort for companies is also significant.

In light of the SEC's auditor independence rules, although auditors may "assist" management in documenting internal control over financial reporting, management must be actively involved in the process and cannot delegate to the auditor management's responsibility to establish and assess internal control.

Material Weakness and Significant Deficiency

The PCAOB auditing standard defines two important terms. "Material weakness," the most serious level of concern, is a subset of "significant deficiency." All material weaknesses are significant deficiencies, but not all significant deficiencies are material weaknesses. Both types must be reported by management to the audit committee and independent auditors. If a material weakness exists as of year-end, the auditors are not permitted to issue a "clean" internal control report. Management's report must describe the material weakness. If the weakness is discovered, fixed and re-tested before year-end, then a clean report may be issued.

A "material weakness" means one or more *significant deficiencies* that result in *more than a remote likelihood* that a *material* misstatement of the annual or interim financial statements will occur and not be detected by management before the financial statements are published. "Remote" means the chance of occurrence is slight and not reasonably possible.

A "significant deficiency" means a deficiency in the design or operation of internal control that adversely affects the company's ability to initiate, authorize, record, process or report external financial data reliably in accordance with generally accepted accounting principles such that there is *more than a remote likelihood* that a misstatement of the annual or interim financial statements that is *more than inconsequential* will occur and not be detected. "Inconsequential" means a reasonable person would conclude the misstatement is clearly immaterial. "Material" means a reasonable investor would consider the information important in the total mix of information available.

The chart below summarizes the two definitions:

	Probability of Problem	Magnitude of Problem	Consequence
Material Weakness (more serious)	More than remote	Material misstatement in financial statements	Adverse report on internal control (public)
Significant Deficiency	More than remote	Significant misstatement in financial statements—less than material but more than inconsequential	Disclosure to audit committee (not public)

Quarterly Evaluation and Disclosure of Internal Control

The SEC rules require management of U.S. public companies, with the participation of the CEO and CFO, to conduct quarterly evaluations of internal control over financial reporting. These quarterly evaluations are in addition to the annual evaluations required in connection with management's internal control report discussed above. Management's quarterly evaluations extend only to changes that materially affect, or are reasonably likely to materially affect, the company's internal control over financial reporting. Management must conduct this evaluation of material changes for each fiscal quarter, including the fourth quarter. That is, the year-end evaluation should include both the evaluation required in connection with management's internal control report and an evaluation of material changes that took place in the fourth quarter. Disclosure about the results of the evaluation must be made to the audit committee. If an annual evaluation reveals a material weakness at year-end, that must be disclosed in management's report on internal control in the annual report. Otherwise, public reporting of a significant deficiency or material weakness is not specifically required. A company should consider the advisability of doing so based on a general materiality analysis.

Although the results of the evaluation need not be publicly disclosed except as described above, any material *change* in internal control over financial reporting is required to be disclosed in the quarterly or annual report for the period in which the change occurs.

Non-U.S. public companies are generally not required to file quarterly reports with the SEC. Accordingly, management of non-U.S. companies is not required to evaluate and disclose material changes on a quarterly basis, even if the company voluntarily furnishes quarterly financial reports on Form 6-K. Instead, management of these non-U.S. companies must evaluate material changes annually, and these companies must disclose material changes in their annual reports filed with the SEC.

Relationship of Disclosure Procedures and Financial Controls

Uncertainties exist in the relationship between disclosure controls and procedures, on the one hand, and internal control over financial reporting, on the other.

The SEC has provided little guidance in this area. According to the SEC, although the two concepts substantively overlap, each may have some elements not included in the other.

With regard to overlap, the SEC has stated that disclosure controls and procedures include those components of internal control over financial reporting that provide reasonable assurances that transactions are recorded as necessary to permit preparation of financial statements in accordance with generally accepted accounting principles.

With regard to non-overlap, the SEC has observed that some companies may design their disclosure controls and procedures to exclude some components of internal control over financial reporting pertaining to the accurate recording of transactions and disposition of assets or to the safeguarding of assets, such as a dual signature requirement for check-signing.

References

Sarbanes-Oxley Act

§ 404

SEC Rules

Rules 13a-15 & 15d-15

Reg. S-K Items 307 & 308

SEC & PCAOB Websites (rules and commentary)

www.sec.gov/rules/final/33-8124.htm
(August 2002 adopting release)

www.sec.gov/rules/final/33-8238.htm
(June 2003 amending release)

www.sec.gov/rules/pcaob/34-49544.htm
   (PCAOB standard relating to audit of internal control)

www.sec.gov/info/accountants/controlfaq1004.htm

www.pcaobus.org/Standards/Staff_Questions_and_
Answers/Auditing_Internal_Control_over_Financial_
Reporting_2004-06-23.pdf

www.pcaobus.org/Standards/Staff_Questions_and_
Answers/Auditing_Internal_Control_over_Financial_
Reporting_2004-10-06.pdf

Chapter 4

Financial Disclosure: Management's Discussion and Analysis

Overview

In the post-Enron disclosure environment, the SEC has moved actively in a number of areas to improve various items of disclosure in the Management's Discussion and Analysis (MD&A), which is the narrative explanation of financial matters required to accompany financial statements in SEC filings. The SEC has indicated that it is also considering future rule proposals or interpretive releases in this area.

SEC's 2003 Guidance Regarding MD&A Disclosure

In late 2003, the SEC published important interpretive guidance regarding MD&A disclosure requirements. The SEC's stated purpose was to assist companies in preparing MD&A disclosure that is easier to follow and understand, and to assist companies in providing information that more completely satisfies the principal objectives of MD&A. The guidance encourages companies to take a fresh look at MD&A with a view to enhancing its quality and highlights four principal areas for improvement:

- the overall presentation of MD&A;

- the focus and content of MD&A, including materiality, analysis, key performance measures and known material trends and uncertainties;

- disclosure regarding liquidity and capital resources; and

- disclosure regarding critical accounting estimates.

The SEC's 2003 interpretive guidance builds on prior SEC guidance regarding MD&A, particularly the SEC's interpretation regarding MD&A issued in 1989. The SEC's 2003 interpretive guidance states that it does not modify existing legal requirements or create new legal requirements. Nevertheless, the guidance can be expected to influence courts in applying the SEC's rules, particularly the MD&A requirements, in light of the SEC's experience as the agency that administers the federal securities laws.

The SEC's 2003 interpretive guidance applies to MD&A disclosure in all SEC disclosure documents, including annual reports, quarterly reports and registration statements, and applies to both U.S. and non-U.S. public companies.

Overall Presentation of MD&A

The SEC's 2003 guidance emphasizes the importance of presenting MD&A disclosure in clear and understandable language. The SEC makes the following specific suggestions:

- include an executive-level overview;

- use a layered approach;

- use tabular presentations;

- use more headings; and

- avoid duplicative disclosure.

Executive-Level Overview

The SEC guidance notes that many companies would benefit from adding an introductory section or executive-level overview that provides context for the remainder of the discussion and analysis. The guidance indicates that a good introduction or overview will provide a balanced, executive-level discussion that identifies the most important matters on which management focuses in evaluating the company's financial condition and operating performance.

The guidance notes that the introduction or overview should not be a duplicative layer of disclosure that merely repeats the more detailed discussion and analysis that follows, nor should it include boilerplate disclaimers and other generic language. The guidance also indicates that, because the matters to be addressed in the introduction do not generally remain static from period to period, the SEC expects that a company's introduction will change over time to remain current.

Layered Approach

The SEC guidance advises companies to consider using a "layered" approach to their MD&A disclosure that emphasizes, within the universe of material information that is disclosed, the information and analysis that is most important. Adding an overview or introduction as noted above is one example provided by the SEC of a layered approach to MD&A disclosure. Another example provided is to begin a section that contains detailed analysis (such as an analysis of period-to-period information) with a statement of the principal factors, trends or other matters that are discussed in more detail in the section.

Tabular Presentation

The SEC guidance advises companies to consider whether the tabular presentation of certain financial and other information might help a reader's understanding of MD&A. For example, a company's MD&A might be clearer if it provides a tabular comparison of its results in different periods, which could include line items and percentage changes as well as other information the company believes is useful, followed by a narrative discussion and analysis of known changes, events, trends, uncertainties and other matters.

Headings

The SEC guidance notes that companies should consider whether the existing headings in its MD&A are helpful to readers' understanding of MD&A and whether additional headings would be helpful.

No Duplicative Disclosure

The SEC guidance encourages companies to avoid unnecessary duplicative disclosure that can tend to overwhelm readers and act as an obstacle to identifying and understanding material matters.

Focus and Content of MD&A

The SEC guidance advises companies to identify and discuss in MD&A the key performance indicators, including non-financial performance indicators, that their management uses to manage the business and that would be material to investors. Non-financial data that may be important to an investor's understanding of a company includes macro-economic information (such as interest rates or economic growth rates and their anticipated trends), industry-specific measures (such as industry metrics and value drivers) or other company-specific measures. The SEC guidance also notes that a company's focus on key performance indicators can be enhanced through the format in which the information is presented and states that the order of the information presented in MD&A need not follow the order set forth in the SEC's MD&A rules if another order of presentation would better facilitate a reader's understanding.

The SEC notes that a company's disclosure should emphasize material information that is required or promotes understanding and deemphasize (or delete) immaterial information. In deciding on the content of MD&A, companies preparing MD&A should evaluate issues presented in previous periods and consider reducing or omitting discussion of those issues that may no longer be material or helpful or revising discussions where a revision would make the continuing relevance of an issue more apparent.

MD&A must identify and analyze trends, demands, commitments, events and uncertainties that will, or are reasonably likely to, have a material effect on financial condition or operating performance. The SEC guidance warns companies against confusing disclosures regarding known material trends and uncertainties in MD&A, which are required, with optional forward-looking information, the disclosure of which is encouraged but not required. The requirement to discuss and analyze known material trends and uncertainties means that companies are *required* to disclose some forward-looking information in MD&A. The SEC's view is that disclosure of a trend, demand, commitment, event or uncertainty is required *unless* a company is able to conclude either that it is not reasonably likely that the trend, uncertainty or other event will occur or come to fruition, or that such trend, uncertainty or other event is not reasonably likely to have a material effect on the company's liquidity, capital resources or results of operations.

The SEC guidance emphasizes that MD&A requires more than a mere restatement of financial statement information in narrative form. The MD&A treatment of known material trends and uncertainties, in particular, must include "analysis" in addition to "discussion."

Liquidity and Capital Resources

The SEC guidance also focuses on the need for disclosure of underlying trends and conditions relating to liquidity and cash flow that are not otherwise readily apparent from the statement of cash flows or other financial statements. The SEC guidance specifically notes that a company should focus on improving disclosure in the areas of cash requirements, sources and uses of cash, debt instruments, guarantees and related covenants and cash management.

Cash Requirements

In order to identify known material cash requirements that should be discussed in MD&A, the SEC guidance advises companies to consider whether the following information would have a material impact on liquidity:

- funds necessary to maintain current operations, complete projects underway and achieve stated objectives or plans;
- commitments for capital or other expenditures; and
- the reasonably likely exposure to future cash requirements associated with known trends or uncertainties, and an indication of the time periods in which resolution of the uncertainties is anticipated.

Consistent with its guidance on the overall presentation of MD&A, the SEC suggests that a company begin its discussion and analysis of cash requirements with the required tabular disclosure of contractual obligations, supplemented with a narrative description of any factors that are material to an understanding of the company's cash requirements.

Sources and Uses of Cash

The MD&A discussion and analysis of liquidity should focus on material changes in operating, investing and financing cash flows and the reasons for those changes. These are the three categories of cash flows presented in the cash flow statement in the financial statements. MD&A should also explain the reasonably likely impact on future cash flows and cash management decisions of any material variability in historical cash flows. Even if cash flows have been consistent, if the underlying sources of those cash flows have materially varied, companies should discuss the reasons for that variability.

Companies should not limit their disclosure of operating cash flows to the manner of presentation in the company's statement of cash flows, but should instead address material changes in the underlying drivers of cash flows.

A company must provide disclosure in MD&A regarding its historical financing arrangements, to the extent material, and their importance to cash flows, including information that is not included in its financial statements. In addition to this historical disclosure, companies may be required to discuss and analyze in MD&A the types of financing that are reasonably likely to be available to the company. This disclosure should also address the types of financing that a company would like to use but that are not reasonably available. The impact of that financing or lack of it on the company's cash position and liquidity may also need to be addressed.

Debt Instruments, Guarantees and Related Covenants

The SEC guidance advises companies to include in MD&A a discussion and analysis of material covenants relating to their outstanding debt, guarantees or contingent obligations. Disclosure is required if a company is reasonably likely to be in breach of those covenants or if the covenants affect its ability to obtain additional debt or equity financing.

Cash Management

Noting that companies generally have some flexibility in deciding when and how to use their cash, the SEC guidance states that a company's MD&A should describe known material trends or uncertainties relating to its decisions on the use of cash.

Critical Accounting Estimates

The SEC also reiterates earlier SEC guidance on the importance of disclosure regarding critical accounting estimates and assumptions. The SEC guidance advises companies to provide disclosure in MD&A of accounting estimates or assumptions where both of the following factors are present:

- the *nature* of the estimates or assumptions is material due to the levels of subjectivity and judgment necessary to account for highly uncertain matters or the susceptibility of such matters to change; and

- the *impact* of the estimates and assumptions on the company's financial condition or operating performance is material.

The SEC emphasizes that this disclosure should supplement, but not duplicate, the company's financial statement notes regarding accounting policies (typically, note 1 to the financial statements), and should provide an analysis of the estimates' and assumptions' sensitivity to change, quantified where this would aid investors.

Additional General MD&A Recommendations

Given the attention being focused on MD&A disclosure, companies may also wish to consider the following:

- ensuring the MD&A is consistent with other public statements of the company, such as earnings releases;

- including a discussion in MD&A about the results of discrete units within an operating segment that contribute differently to results within the segment;

- arranging discussion sessions about the draft MD&A and broadening participation in these discussion sessions to include inside or outside securities counsel and the outside auditors;

- providing a draft MD&A to the audit committee for its review prior to filing the company's annual report with the SEC; and

- taking into account the SEC's comments contained in its 2002 review of the MD&A disclosures of the Fortune 500 companies, discussed in chapter 6.

Off-Balance-Sheet Disclosures

The SEC also has rules requiring U.S. and non-U.S. public companies to provide an explanation of their off-balance-sheet arrangements. This explanation must appear in a separately captioned subsection of the MD&A.

The impact of the off-balance-sheet disclosure rules was moderated by the adoption of a stricter accounting standard in the same year (2003), which requires consolidation in more circumstances of special purpose entities. The off-balance-sheet disclosure rules do not apply to consolidated entities.

The definition of "off-balance-sheet arrangements" contained in the rules captures a broad range of arrangements involving guarantees, retained or contingent interests, derivative instruments and variable interests in unconsolidated entities. Relatively detailed disclosure about the purpose and significance of these off-balance-sheet arrangements is required by the rules. Some cross-referencing to financial statement footnote disclosure is permitted, but the substance of the relevant disclosures contained in the footnotes is required to be integrated into the off-balance-sheet disclosure subsection of MD&A.

U.S. and non-U.S. public companies are also required to include in MD&A a table summarizing certain categories of contractual obligations.

Critical Accounting Policies

Shortly before enactment of the SOA in 2002, the SEC proposed additional MD&A disclosure requirements regarding a company's critical accounting policies. The proposals have not been adopted as rules, but in its 2003 MD&A guidance the SEC endorsed the spirit of the proposals as a matter that should currently be addressed in MD&A in a critical accounting estimates discussion, as previously discussed on page 45.

Under the first part of the 2002 proposal, a company would have to identify in its annual report MD&A those accounting estimates reflected in its financial statements that both required it to make assumptions about matters that were "highly uncertain" at the time of estimation and that were sufficiently important. An estimate would be considered sufficiently important if different estimates that the company reasonably could have used in the current period, or changes in the accounting estimates that are reasonably likely to occur from period to period, would have a material impact on the presentation of the company's financial condition, changes in financial condition or results of operations. The proposal would also require that the effect of changes in these critical accounting estimates be quantified. U.S. companies would also be required to update information in their quarterly reports.

Under the second part of the proposal, at any time a company initially adopted an accounting policy having a material impact on its financial presentation, the company would have to disclose the events that gave rise to the adoption as well as the qualitative (but not quantitative) impact of the adoption and the choices the company had among accounting principles.

These two aspects of the proposal have not become requirements in the full detail proposed, but, as previously noted, the SEC does expect companies to address critical accounting policies in MD&A and to look to the proposals as guides to the types of information the SEC considers important.

References

Sarbanes-Oxley Act

§ 401(a)

SEC Rules

Reg. S-K Item 303

SEC Website (rules and commentary)

www.sec.gov/rules/interp/33-8350.htm

Chapter 5

Disclosure of Non-GAAP Financial Measures

Overview

In response to a perception that the use by public companies of financial measures that are not calculated and presented in accordance with generally accepted accounting principles (GAAP) could mislead and confuse investors, the SEC adopted rules, as directed by the Sarbanes-Oxley Act, to:

- regulate the use of these so-called "non-GAAP financial measures" in public announcements and other public disclosures by U.S. and non-U.S. public companies;

- impose additional limitations on the use of non-GAAP financial measures in SEC filings by U.S. and non-U.S. public companies; and

- require U.S. public companies to furnish to the SEC on Form 8-K, within four business days, earnings releases or other announcements containing material non-public financial information about completed annual or quarterly fiscal periods.

Required Reconciliation in Public Announcements—Regulation G

The SEC's disclosure regime under the SOA regarding the use of non-GAAP financial measures is principally set forth in a set of rules called Regulation G. These rules apply to all public disclosures made on behalf of a public company, whether or not contained in an SEC filing.

Definition of a "Non-GAAP Financial Measure"

A "non-GAAP financial measure" is a numerical measure of a company's financial performance, financial position or cash flows that is computed differently than the most directly comparable measure calculated and presented in accordance with GAAP. The difference could result from excluding amounts that the GAAP measure includes, or including amounts that are not part of the GAAP measure. A GAAP measure means a line item in the statement of income, balance sheet or statement of cash flows of the company or a subcomponent of a line item. It may also be an item from the financial statement footnotes.

Examples of non-GAAP financial measures identified by the SEC include:

- EBITDA (that is, earnings before interest, taxes, depreciation and amortization);

- measures of operating income that exclude one or more "non-recurring" items;

- free cash flow;

- funds from operations; and

- segment information computed differently from the GAAP segment information in the financial statement footnotes.

Whether or not listed by the SEC, a measure would be a non-GAAP financial measure if it meets the definition.

Non-GAAP financial measures must be *financial* in order to be subject to the rules. The rules do not apply to operating and other statistical measures (such as square footage and number of employees), and ratios or measures that are calculated using only financial measures calculated in accordance with GAAP and operating or other measures that are not non-GAAP financial measures. One example is same store sales based on GAAP sales. The rules also do not apply to financial measures required to be disclosed by GAAP, by SEC rules or by any other system of regulation of a government or governmental authority or self-regulatory organization that is applicable to the public company.

Required GAAP Reconciliation

Under the SEC rules, whenever a public company discloses publicly, whether orally or in writing, any material information that includes a non-GAAP financial measure, the company is required to include in that disclosure:

- a presentation of the most directly comparable financial measure calculated and presented in accordance with GAAP, such as earnings or cash flows reported in GAAP financial statements; and

• a reconciliation of the non-GAAP financial measure presented with the most directly comparable financial measure or measures calculated and presented in accordance with GAAP. The reconciliation must be made by schedule or other clearly understandable method.

For historical measures, the reconciliation must be quantitative, and no exceptions are permitted. For prospective measures, the reconciliation should also be quantitative, but only if that can be done without unreasonable effort. The SEC rules also require that a non-GAAP financial measure, taken together with the accompanying information, not be materially false or materially misleading.

If a non-GAAP financial measure is released orally, telephonically, in a webcast, by broadcast or by similar means, the public company may provide the required accompanying information by posting it on its website if it also discloses during the presentation the location and availability of the required accompanying information. The posting must occur on or before the broadcast. The SEC has encouraged companies to provide ongoing website access to this information and has suggested that companies provide access to this information for at least a twelve-month period.

Expanded Disclosure of Non-GAAP Information for SEC Filings

If the non-GAAP financial information is contained in an SEC filing, the SEC rules require expanded disclosure beyond that required for press releases and other public announcements that are not filed with the SEC. The rules also prohibit altogether the use of some types of non-GAAP measures in SEC filings.

Required Disclosures in SEC Filings

In addition to the GAAP reconciliation required for all public announcements, as discussed above, an SEC filing that contains non-

GAAP financial information must also meet the following requirements:

- the most directly comparable financial measure calculated and
  presented in accordance with GAAP must be presented with
  equal or greater prominence, rather than merely accompanying
  the non-GAAP measure;

- there must be a statement describing the *reasons* why management believes the non-GAAP financial measure provides useful
  information to investors; and

- to the extent material and not already covered in the statement
  in the previous bullet, there must be a statement disclosing the
  purposes for which management uses the non-GAAP financial
  measure presented.

The SEC has stated that the required statements of the purposes
for which management uses the non-GAAP financial measure and the
usefulness of the information should be clear and understandable.
The statements should not be "boilerplate," but should instead be
specific to the non-GAAP financial measure used and the specifics of
the company and industry.

If the two required statements are included in the annual report on
Form 10-K of a U.S. public company and those statements remain
current, there is no need to include the same statements in a subsequent securities offering filing or quarterly report on Form 10-Q that
includes the non-GAAP financial measure. The same applies if a non-
U.S. public company includes the two required statements in its annual report on Form 20-F and makes a subsequent SEC filing during
the current year that contains a non-GAAP financial measure.

Prohibited Disclosures in SEC Filings

There are three types of non-GAAP financial measures that are
prohibited in SEC filings:

- performance measures that exclude recurring items;

- liquidity measures that exclude cash items; and

- non-GAAP measures of any kind that are located within the financial statements.

With respect to the first of these prohibited measures, the SEC rules prohibit adjusting a non-GAAP performance measure in an SEC filing to eliminate or smooth items "identified" as nonrecurring, infrequent or unusual that have occurred in the prior two years or are reasonably likely to recur in the next two years. For example, the rules prohibit presenting a measure called "recurring income" if any of the items excluded from that measure has occurred within the prior two years.

With respect to the second of these prohibited measures, the SEC rules also prohibit public companies from using a non-GAAP liquidity measure that excludes charges or liabilities that required, or will require, cash settlement, or would have required cash settlement absent an ability to settle in another manner. The SEC has explicitly exempted EBIT and EBITDA from this prohibition, but only if computed in the manner described by the SEC. The SEC allowed the exception because of the widespread and recognized existing use of these measures. Companies are still required to reconcile EBIT and EBITDA to their most directly comparable GAAP financial measures and explain why investors would find them useful in the context in which these measures are presented. EBIT or EBITDA measures computed differently than in the manner described by the SEC are prohibited in SEC filings if they are used as a liquidity measure and exclude a cash settlement item.

Finally, the SEC rules prohibit companies from presenting non-GAAP financial measures in their GAAP financial statements or related footnotes, or on the face of pro forma financial information required by applicable SEC rules. Companies are also prohibited from using titles or descriptions of non-GAAP financial measures that are the same as, or confusingly similar to, titles or descriptions used for GAAP financial measures.

Form 8-K Furnishing of Earnings Releases by U.S. Public Companies

U.S. public companies must furnish to the SEC on Form 8-K earnings press releases or other announcements disclosing material non-public information about completed annual or quarterly fiscal periods. The Form 8-K is due four business days after the public announcement (prior to August 23, 2004, the deadline was five business days).

Announcements That Are Covered

The 8-K rule covers *any* public announcement by a U.S. public company, whether oral or written, containing material non-public earnings or balance sheet information about completed annual or quarterly periods, *even if the announcement contains no non-GAAP financial measures.*

If the disclosure is made in quarterly reports filed on Form 10-Q or annual reports filed on Form 10-K, no Form 8-K is required. The 8-K requirement also does not apply to earnings estimates for *future* ongoing fiscal periods if published in a stand-alone disclosure and not combined with material non-public information regarding a completed annual or quarterly fiscal period. Mere repetition of previously publicly disclosed information in a different form would not trigger a new 8-K submission requirement, unless accompanied by additional or updated material non-public historical financial information.

It should be noted that earnings releases furnished on Form 8-K are not automatically incorporated by reference into a company's securities offering registration statements. The SEC has also confirmed that late submission of earnings releases on Form 8-K does not cause the company to lose eligibility for Form S-3, the short form used by larger companies for shelf registration and other securities offerings and that relies on disclosure in existing Form 10-K, 10-Q and 8-K filings.

Relationship of 8-K Requirement to Other Non-GAAP Rules

Earnings releases that contain non-GAAP financial measures and are furnished to the SEC on Form 8-K are subject to some, but not all, of the special requirements relating to use of non-GAAP financial measures in SEC filings. These earnings release 8-Ks are required to include a reconciliation to the most directly comparable GAAP financial measure. In addition, the comparable GAAP financial measure must be presented with greater or equal prominence, and the company must include the required statements of the purposes for which management uses the non-GAAP financial measure and the usefulness of the information. However, these additional disclosures may be placed in the Form 8-K and do not need to be included in the earnings release itself.

Furthermore, the SEC has clarified that the prohibited disclosures and other limitations applicable to SEC filings, discussed in the section "Prohibited Disclosures in SEC Filings," beginning on page 53, would not apply to a Form 8-K furnished under the earnings release rule.

Forty-Eight-Hour Exception

The SEC rules permit a company to avoid making a Form 8-K submission covering non-public information disclosed in a follow-up earnings release conference call, if the company meets the following conditions:

- the follow-up disclosure is made orally, telephonically, by webcast, by broadcast or by similar means;

- the follow-up disclosure initially occurs within forty-eight hours after a written press release or announcement;

- the original release or announcement has been furnished on Form 8-K by the time of the follow-up disclosure;

- the follow-up presentation is accessible to the public by dial-in conference call, webcast or similar technology;

- the financial and statistical information contained in the follow-up presentation is provided on the company's website, together with any additional information that would be required under the SEC rules regarding non-GAAP financial information; and

- the follow-up presentation was announced by a widely disseminated press release instructing when and how to access the presentation and stating the location on the company's website where the information would be available.

Given the forty-eight-hour deadline in the list of conditions, the 8-K exemption for the follow-up presentation is available only to companies that furnish the required earnings release Form 8-K to the SEC in advance of the general four-business-day deadline.

Limited Exceptions for Business Combinations and Non-U.S. Public Companies

Business Combinations

The SEC rules contain a limited exception for non-GAAP financial measures included in disclosure relating to a business combination transaction. The exception is available only for disclosures covered by specific SEC rules relating to pre-commencement communications in business combinations.

Non-U.S. Public Companies

The SEC non-GAAP rules contain a limited exception for announcements made by a non-U.S. public company outside the United States. In addition, materials submitted on Form 6-K are subject only to the general non-GAAP rules applicable to all public announcements and not to the expanded disclosure requirements and prohibitions for non-GAAP information in SEC filings, if the 6-K information is not incorporated by reference into the non-U.S.

company's securities offering registration statement, prospectus or annual report.

References

Sarbanes-Oxley Act

§ 401(b)

SEC Rules

Reg. G & Reg. S-K Item 10

SEC Website (rules and commentary)

www.sec.gov/rules/final/33-8176.htm

www.sec.gov/divisions/corpfin/faqs/nongaapfaq.htm

COMPLIANCE CHECKLIST:
Non-GAAP Financial Measures

	Public Statements	Earnings Release & 8-K	Other SEC Filings
Must Include			
Nearest GAAP measure	✓	✓ & Equal or greater prominence	✓ & Equal or greater prominence
Reconciliation to nearest GAAP measure	✓	✓	✓
Explanation of purpose for non-GAAP measure and why useful to investors		✓ (in 8-K)	✓
Must Exclude			
Performance measures that exclude recurring items (in other words, items occurring in past 2 years or likely in next 2 years)			✓
Liquidity measures that exclude cash items (but EBIT and EBITDA computed in the SEC manner are permitted)			✓
Any non-GAAP measure in financial statements			✓

GAAP = generally accepted accounting principles
EBIT = earnings before interest and taxes
EBITDA = earnings before interest, taxes, depreciation and amortization

Chapter 6

Real-Time Disclosures

Overview

The SEC is requiring more and earlier disclosures by U.S. public
companies. They must promptly disclose the occurrence of specified
events that the SEC believes are "clearly material," including commencement or termination of material contracts, new financial obligations, material write-offs, restatements and changes in directors or
principal officers. The disclosure must be made in a Form 8-K filed
with the SEC within four business days of the event, starting in August 2004. Large U.S. companies must also file their annual Form
10-K reports and quarterly Form 10-Q reports within earlier deadlines than in 2002 and prior years.

Expanded Form 8-K Disclosure Requirements

Overview

The SEC has added many new events to its Form 8-K current event
disclosure requirements for U.S. public companies, effective in August 2004. These new requirements stem from a June 2002 SEC proposal that predated the Sarbanes-Oxley Act. The SEC also shortened
the Form 8-K reporting deadline for all reportable events to four
business days after the occurrence of the event triggering a disclosure
requirement, with no extension available, from the previous five-
business-day and fifteen-calendar-day deadlines.

The rules do not apply to non-U.S. public companies, which do not use Form 8-K.

The new 8-K events are:

- entry into or termination of a material agreement;

- creation of a material obligation that is either direct or arises contingently out of an off-balance-sheet arrangement;

- occurrence of an event of default or event of acceleration regarding a financial obligation;

- commitment to exit an activity or dispose of an asset that will result in a material write-off under generally accepted accounting principles, such as a plant closing;

- decision to write down materially the value of an asset, including a goodwill impairment;

- notice from a stock exchange regarding failure to satisfy listing standards;

- decision to restate financial statements; and

- departure or election of a director or senior executive officer.

The following events have been moved into current reporting on Form 8-K. They were previously subject to quarterly reporting on Form 10-Q or 10-K:

- sales of equity securities in a private placement or other unregistered transaction exceeding 1% of the outstanding securities;

- material modification to the rights of holders of equity, debt or other securities; and

- amendment to articles of incorporation or by-laws.

The following events have been retained as required disclosures in Form 8-K, but are subject to the shorter four-business-day deadline:

- bankruptcy or receivership;

- completion of purchase or sale of significant assets (financial statements of an acquired business and related pro forma information may continue to be filed on a delayed basis, though);

- publication of an earnings release or other announcement of historical results;

- change in auditor;

- change in control;

- temporary suspension of employee transfers under 401(k) or other benefit plans; and

- amendment to or waiver of the code of ethics for senior financial officers.

Entry into a Material Definitive Agreement

The material definitive agreements subject to this 8-K reporting requirement include the same types of agreements previously required to be filed as exhibits to a company's periodic reports on Forms 10-K and 10-Q, including management-related agreements. Non-binding letters of intent are not covered.

Termination of a Material Definitive Agreement

A company is required to disclose on Form 8-K the termination of a material definitive agreement if that termination is material to the company. No disclosure is required if an agreement expires on its stated termination date or as a result of completion by all parties of their obligations.

Creation of a Direct Financial Obligation or an Obligation Under an Off-Balance-Sheet Arrangement

A company is required to disclose on Form 8-K whenever it becomes obligated under a material direct financial obligation, including a long-term debt obligation, capital or operating lease obligation or a short-term debt obligation not in the ordinary course of business. Disclosure is also triggered when a company becomes directly or contingently liable for a material obligation arising out of an off-balance-sheet arrangement. There is an exception for obligations consisting of securities sold in an SEC-registered public offering.

Triggering Events That Accelerate or Increase a Direct Financial Obligation or an Obligation Under an Off-Balance-Sheet Arrangement

A company is required to disclose triggering events, such as an event of default or event of acceleration, if either of the following results from the event:

- a direct financial obligation of the company is increased or becomes accelerated, or an obligation of the company arising under an off-balance-sheet arrangement is increased or becomes accelerated; or

- a contingent obligation of the company arising out of an off-balance-sheet arrangement becomes a direct financial obligation of the company.

Costs Associated with Exit or Disposal Activities

A company is required to disclose when it has committed to a plan to exit an activity or dispose of a long-lived asset that will result in material charges (write-offs) under generally accepted accounting principles. Committing to any other course of action that will result in a material write-off would also trigger disclosure. The disclosure must include a good-faith estimate of the charge, broken out by major type (such as one-time termination benefits, contract termination costs and other associated costs) and an estimate of the amount of the charge that will result in future cash expenditures. If an estimate is unavailable at the time of filing, the company must disclose within four days of formulating one.

Material Impairments

A company must disclose a decision to record a material charge (write-down) for an asset impairment, including an impairment of the value of securities or goodwill. This disclosure must include an estimated amount of the impairment charge and an estimated amount of the charge that will result in future cash expenditures. No disclosure is required to the extent the decision is made in connection with the preparation of quarterly or annual financial statements, as will usually be the case, and the charge is disclosed in the Form 10-Q or 10-K for that period.

Notice of Delisting or Failure to Satisfy Listing Standards; Transfers of Listings

A company must report a delisting notice from the stock exchange (or the Nasdaq Stock Market) on which its common stock is listed, as well as any company-initiated delisting action, such as transfer to another exchange. A company must also disclose receipt of a public reprimand letter or similar communication from the exchange stating that the company violated an exchange rule or standard. In addition, the company must publicly disclose any notification it gives to the exchange that the company is aware of material noncompliance with a listing rule, including a violation of the governance requirements described in chapters 7, 8 and 9. The exchanges generally require such a notice to be given promptly upon an executive officer's becoming aware of the noncompliance.

Unregistered Sales of Equity Securities

The company must disclose unregistered sales of equity securities since its last periodic report or its last 8-K disclosure if the sales exceed 1% of its outstanding securities. This disclosure was previously required only quarterly. Sales below the 1% level must continue to be disclosed quarterly on Forms 10-Q and 10-K.

Material Modification to Rights of Security Holders

Disclosure of material modification to the rights of security holders, previously required quarterly on Forms 10-Q and 10-K, has been moved to Form 8-K and therefore is subject to four-business-day reporting.

Restatement of Previously Issued Financial Statements

A company must disclose a decision that its previously issued financial statements should no longer be relied upon due to error, which will require restatement. Similar disclosure is required if the company's current or former auditor withdraws a previously issued audit report or completed interim review.

A Director Departs or Declines to Stand for Reelection

Disclosure is required when a director retires, resigns, is removed or declines to stand for reelection for any reason. If the director resigns due to a disagreement known to management or is removed for cause, that fact must also be disclosed. Previously, disclosure was required only if the director provided a letter to the company describing the disagreement and requesting public disclosure.

Principal Officers Retire, Resign or Are Terminated

A company must disclose when its principal executive officer, president, principal financial officer, principal accounting officer, principal operating officer or any person serving in an equivalent position retires, resigns or is terminated from that position. No explanation need be given, even if the officer's termination involves a disagreement.

A New Director Is Elected or New Principal Officer Is Appointed

A company must disclose the election of a new director, unless the election occurs at an annual or special shareholders meeting. A company must also disclose the appointment of a new principal executive officer, president, principal financial officer, principal accounting officer, principal operating officer or person serving an equivalent function.

Amendments to Articles of Incorporation or Bylaws; Change in Fiscal Year

Any amendment to a company's articles of incorporation or bylaws must be disclosed, as well as a change in its fiscal year. Amendments approved by shareholders need not be disclosed, since they would already have been disclosed in a proxy statement.

Other 8-K Requirements

The previous Form 8-K disclosable events have been retained. These include commencement of bankruptcy or receivership proceedings involving the company, completion of a business combination involving a change of control or involving the purchase or sale of significant assets and a company's change of auditor. The permissibility of delayed filing of financial statements and *pro forma* information for business combinations has been retained.

In addition to the above, the SEC requires U.S. public companies to disclose on Form 8-K earnings releases, discussed in chapter 5, codes of ethics amendments and waivers, discussed in chapter 9, and benefit plan blackout notices, discussed in chapter 10.

Shortened Deadlines for 10-K and 10-Q

Four-Year Phase-In Period

The SEC has shortened the filing deadlines for annual and quarterly reports filed by large U.S. public companies on Forms 10-K and 10-Q. For a standard calendar year filer, the 2005 Form 10-K will be due March 1, 2006, which is sixty days after the end of the year (rather than ninety days for the 2002 Form 10-K). In 2006, Forms 10-Q will be due thirty-five days after the end of each quarter (rather than forty-five days for the 2003 Forms 10-Q). Reports for earlier periods are due on phased-in shortened deadlines, representing an overall phase-in period of four years, including a one-year hiatus in shortening the deadlines to give larger companies more time for their first internal control audits, discussed in chapter 3. For smaller U.S. public companies, the previous ninety- and forty-five-day deadlines remain unchanged.

Enhanced Disclosure Regarding Website Access to Periodic and Current Reports

Large U.S. public companies must disclose in their annual reports on Form 10-K whether their 10-K, 10-Q and 8-K reports are available on their Internet websites.

A company that does not make its reports available in this manner must disclose the reasons and disclose whether it will voluntarily provide free electronic or paper copies.

The SEC has encouraged companies to provide ongoing website access to their reports and suggested that, at a minimum, companies provide website access to their previous reports for at least a twelve-month period.

Increased SEC Review of Public Filings

Mandatory Three-Year Review

The SOA requires the SEC to review a public company's annual, quarterly and other SEC reports at least once every three years. Although the SEC has made no official comment about this mandate under the SOA, its staff has indicated that the depth of review of a particular company's filings may depend on the presence of factors indicative of greater risk of disclosure problems. The SEC staff has also indicated informally that the largest public companies should expect their filings to be reviewed every year.

Special SEC Review in 2002 of Fortune 500 Companies

In 2002, the SEC staff conducted a special review of the annual reports and quarterly reports of the 500 largest U.S. public companies filed that year, with a focus on financial disclosure. Some non-U.S. public companies' filings were also reviewed. In February 2003, the SEC's Division of Corporation Finance issued a report summarizing the principal subjects of staff comment on the periodic reports of these so-called Fortune 500 companies.

The SEC report identified the following principal subjects where improvement in companies' disclosure was needed:

- general approach to the disclosure in management's discussion and analysis;

- critical accounting policy disclosure;

- financial information not calculated or presented in accordance with generally accepted accounting principles;

- revenue recognition;

- restructuring charges;

- impairment charges;

- pension plans;

- segment reporting;

- securitized financial assets and off-balance-sheet arrangements; and

- environmental and product liability disclosures.

Public Release of Comment and Response Letters

On June 24, 2004, the SEC announced a new policy to make publicly available comment letters issued by its Divisions of Corporation Finance and Investment Management on public filings, as well as the non-confidential portions of issuer response letters. The new policy applies to comment and response letters relating to public filings made after August 1, 2004. Comment and response letters are made publicly available forty-five days or more following completion of the SEC staff's filing review.

The new policy does not appear to change the procedures for requesting confidential treatment of information submitted to the SEC in response letters. In order to claim confidential treatment, issuers should submit two response letters to the SEC staff—a complete copy including confidential information, submitted in paper form and accompanied by a request for confidential treatment, and a redacted electronic copy with confidential information removed, submitted via EDGAR.

References

Sarbanes-Oxley Act

§§ 408 & 409

SEC Website (rules and commentary)

www.sec.gov/rules/final/33-8128.htm

www.sec.gov/rules/final/33-8400.htm

www.sec.gov/divisions/corpfin/fortune500rep.htm

www.sec.gov/news/press/2004-89.htm

Chapter 7

Governance:
Board of Directors

Overview

Neither the Sarbanes-Oxley Act nor SEC rules contain any requirements relating to public companies' boards of directors per se, the only exception being the audit committee requirements discussed in chapter 8. However, as part of the corporate governance reform efforts surrounding the enactment of the SOA, the New York Stock Exchange, Nasdaq Stock Market and American Stock Exchange added many requirements to their corporate governance listing standards, including heightened standards relating to director independence.

These stock exchange rules:

- require majority-independent boards of directors;

- tighten the definition of "independent" by setting forth specific bright-line tests and otherwise requiring an affirmative board determination of independence;

- require independent or non-management directors to meet regularly in executive sessions without management present;

- increase the duties and responsibilities of the independent directors in the areas of director nominations and senior management compensation; and

- expand audit committee powers and requirements.

While the thrust of the rules of each stock exchange is the same, the specifics differ. The NYSE and Nasdaq requirements are described below. The Amex requirements are generally the same as those of Nasdaq.

Director Independence

NYSE Director Independence Rules

Covered NYSE Companies

The NYSE corporate governance rules apply to all U.S. public companies with common stock listed on the NYSE, other than SEC-registered closed-end funds and some other types of special purpose entities.

Companies whose majority voting power is held by an individual, group or another company, referred to as "controlled companies," are exempt from the majority-independent board requirement and the requirements for independent nomination and compensation committees.

The NYSE rules exempt listed non-U.S. public companies from the NYSE corporate governance requirements. Instead, non-U.S. listed companies must disclose any significant ways in which their home-country corporate governance practices differ from those followed by U.S. listed companies under the NYSE listing standards. The SEC audit committee requirements described in chapter 8 nevertheless apply to non-U.S. listed companies. These non-U.S. companies must notify the NYSE if they become aware they have not complied with the audit committee requirements or the disclosure about differences in home country practices.

Majority-Independent Board

The NYSE requires that a listed company's board of directors have a majority of independent directors. The names of the independent directors must be disclosed in the annual proxy statement.

Executive Sessions of Non-Management Directors

The NYSE requires that directors who are not officers of a listed company, referred to as "non-management directors," meet at regularly scheduled executive sessions without management present. A company must disclose in its annual proxy statement the name of the director who will preside at these sessions or the procedure by which the presiding director is chosen for each session.

A listed company must disclose a method for interested parties to communicate directly with the presiding director or with the non-management directors as a group.

Bright-Line NYSE Director Independence Tests

Under the NYSE rules, directors who have had any of the following relationships with a listed company are not considered independent until three years after the end of the relationship:

- the director is an executive officer of the company;

- the director receives more than $100,000 per year in direct compensation from the company, other than director and committee fees and pension;

- the director is currently an executive officer of another company that makes payments to or receives payments from the listed company for property or services in an amount that exceeds 2% of the director's company's annual consolidated gross revenues (if the 2% is also over $1 million);

- there is a compensation committee interlock—in other words, the director is an executive officer of another company where one of the listed company's present executives serves on that company's compensation committee; or

- the director is affiliated with or employed by a present or former internal or external auditor of the listed company.

In addition, a director is not independent if any immediate family member has any of the above relationships with the listed company, except that a family member's employment by an auditor is only considered if the family member is employed in a professional, rather than a clerical, capacity. Charitable organizations are not covered by the 2% revenue test. Instead disclosure in the listed company's proxy statement is required if annual contributions exceed the 2% level.

The above bright-line tests for director independence under the NYSE rules apply for a look-back period of three years. However, until November 4, 2004 (which is the end of the first year following the SEC's approval of the NYSE rules), companies applying these tests are required to look back only one year for the existence of disqualifying relationships. Thereafter, the three-year look-back will spring into effect, and directors considered independent under the one-year look-back will cease to be independent if they have independence-impairing relationships in the earlier years.

Affirmative Independence Determinations

The NYSE requires that, even if a director does not fail any of the bright-line tests, the board of directors must affirmatively determine, based on all relevant facts and circumstances, that each independent director has no material relationship with the company, either directly or as a partner, shareholder or officer of a company that has a relationship with the listed company.

Disclosure of Categorical Standards

The basis for the independence determination regarding each director must be disclosed in the company's annual proxy statement. Under a permitted alternative, which most companies will utilize, the company may disclose standards in various categories of relationships that are applied in making the determination and state that a director satisfies those standards.

For example, a company could disclose that contributions by the listed company amounting to less than 1% of a charity's annual revenues will not be considered to impair the independence of a company director employed by that charity. If the company has a director whose charity receives ½% of its revenues from the listed company's contributions, no disclosure about that specific director's relationship would be required, because it is covered by the generic disclosure.

Nasdaq Director Independence Rules

Covered Nasdaq Companies

The Nasdaq corporate governance rules apply to all entities with stock listed on the Nasdaq Stock Market, other than some types of special purpose entities. Like the NYSE, a "controlled company"— where the majority voting power is held by an entity or group—is exempt from the majority-independent board requirement and the requirements for independent nominations and compensation committees.

Unlike the NYSE, Nasdaq has not adopted an automatic, across-the-board exemption for non-U.S. public companies; rather, Nasdaq-listed non-U.S. companies must apply to Nasdaq for specific exemptions from the corporate governance requirements.

Majority-Independent Board

Nasdaq requires that the board of directors have a majority of independent directors. Similar to the NYSE, Nasdaq also provides an exemption from this requirement for so-called "controlled companies," as discussed above.

Executive Sessions of Independent Directors

Nasdaq requires that independent directors meet at regularly scheduled executive sessions at which only independent directors are present, at least twice a year, in conjunction with regularly scheduled board meetings.

Bright-Line Nasdaq Director Independence Tests

Under the Nasdaq rules, the following relationships are considered bars to independence until three years after the end of the relationship:

- the director is employed by the listed company or any parent or subsidiary;
- the director accepts any payments from the listed company or any parent or subsidiary in excess of $60,000 per year, other than compensation for board service and retirement plans;
- the director is an executive officer or equivalent of any organization that makes payments to or receives payments from the listed company for property or services that exceed 5% of the recipient's annual consolidated gross revenues (if the 5% is also over $200,000);
- there is a compensation committee interlock—in other words, the director is an executive officer of a company that has an executive officer of the listed company on its compensation committee; or
- a director is or was a partner of the listed company's outside auditor, or an employee of the outside auditor who worked on the listed company's audit.

In addition, a director is not independent if any immediate family member has any of the above relationships with the listed company, except that a family member's employment by the listed company is only considered if the family member is an executive officer of the listed company. Unlike the NYSE, Nasdaq does include charitable organizations in the 5% revenue test.

The above bright-line bars to director independence under the Nasdaq rules apply for a three-year look-back period. Unlike the NYSE, there is no transition one-year look-back.

Affirmative Independence Determinations

Like the NYSE, Nasdaq requires that the board of directors affirmatively determine for each director that the director has no relationship that would interfere with the exercise of independent judgment in carrying out the director's responsibilities.

Audit Committee

Audit committee requirements of the stock exchanges and the SEC are discussed in chapter 8.

Nominating/Corporate Governance Committee

NYSE Requirements

The NYSE independence rules require each listed company to establish a nominating/corporate governance committee composed entirely of independent directors. The committee is responsible for identifying and recommending the annual director slate to be voted on by shareholders. The committee must also recommend corporate governance principles. The nominating/corporate governance committee must have a written charter that addresses these and other matters. The charter must be posted on the company's website. The responsibilities of the nominating/corporate governance committee can be allocated to one or more other committees composed entirely of independent directors, but those committees must also have written charters. The name of the committee may be selected by the company.

So-called "controlled companies," discussed on page 75, are exempt from the requirement to have a nominating/corporate governance committee. Also, in cases where a company is legally required by contract to provide a third party with the ability to nominate directors, the NYSE rule excepts those directors from the purview of the nominating/corporate governance committee.

Nasdaq Requirements

Nasdaq requires that the nomination of the directors of each listed company be determined by either a majority of the independent directors or a nominations committee comprised solely of independent directors. As with the NYSE, this requirement does not apply to so-called "controlled companies" or in cases where the right to nominate a director legally belongs to a third party. It also does not apply where a company has a noncomplying director nomination structure that predated the rule (that is, was in place before November 2003). Companies must adopt a formal written charter or board resolution, as applicable, addressing the nominations process.

Under exceptional and limited circumstances, one committee member may be non-independent, but must nevertheless not be a company employee nor a family member of an employee and may not serve for more than two years.

Proxy Statement Disclosure Regarding Nominating Committee Functions and Communications Between Security Holders and Boards of Directors

Under SEC rules, U.S. public companies, even non-listed public companies, must include the following disclosure regarding the director nomination process in their annual proxy statements:

- whether a company has a nominating committee and, if not, the reasons why it does not and how director nominations are determined;
- the nominating committee charter;
- the independence of nominating committee members;
- whether the nominating committee has a policy regarding candidates put forward by shareholders and, if so, its process for considering candidates recommended by shareholders;
- the nominating committee's process for identifying and evaluating director nominees;
- minimum qualifications that the committee seeks in director nominees;

- the categories of persons or entities who recommended a director nominee;

- the function performed by any third party engaged to assist in the process of identifying or evaluating candidates; and

- if a candidate has been recommended by a 5% shareholder, disclosure whether the nominating committee chose to nominate the candidate and identification of the candidate and the recommending 5% shareholder.

If a U.S. public company does not have a nominating or similar committee, the SEC rules require the company to disclose the basis for the view of the board of directors that it is appropriate for the company not to have a nominating committee and to identify each director who participates in the consideration of director nominees.

Shareholder Communications with the Board

SEC rules also require that U.S. public companies disclose in their annual proxy statements:

- whether a company has a process for communications by shareholders with the board and, if not, the reasons why it does not;

- the procedure for sending shareholder communications to the board and, if applicable, to individual directors;

- whether those communications are screened and, if so, how; and

- the company's policy with regard to board members' attendance at annual meetings and a statement of the number of directors who attended the prior year's meeting.

Corporate Governance Guidelines

The NYSE corporate governance rules require each listed company to adopt and post on its website a set of corporate governance guidelines, which must address a list of matters. Nasdaq does not have a similar requirement.

Compensation Committee

NYSE Requirements

The NYSE requires each listed company to establish a compensation committee composed entirely of independent directors. The committee is responsible for CEO performance evaluation and compensation. It also advises the board on other executive compensation and benefit plan matters. The compensation committee must have a written charter that addresses these and other matters. The charter must be posted on the company's website. The rules permit the committee's responsibilities to be allocated to one or more other committees composed entirely of independent directors, but those committees must also have written charters. So-called "controlled companies" are exempt from the compensation committee requirement.

Nasdaq Requirements

Nasdaq requires that the compensation of the CEO and officers of each listed company be determined or recommended to the board by either a majority of the independent directors or a compensation committee composed solely of independent directors. Nasdaq expressly prohibits the CEO from being present during voting or deliberations concerning his or her salary.

The compensation committee requirement does not apply to so-called "controlled companies." Also, under circumstances similar to Nasdaq's exception for the composition of the nominations committee discussed on page 80, one non-independent director can be appointed to the compensation committee.

Proposed SEC Rules on Direct Shareholder Access to Company Proxy Materials to Nominate Directors

The SEC proposed controversial rules in October 2003 that would permit shareholders of U.S. public companies to make competing director nominations in the company's annual proxy statement. As of this writing, the rule has not yet become effective, and it is uncertain whether it will. If it does, the rule will likely be different in its final form than as proposed. Under the proposal, if either of the triggering events described below occurs, significant shareholders or groups of shareholders may nominate at least one and up to three directors, depending on the size of the company's board. The nominating procedure would be triggered by:

- the receipt of withhold votes at a prior meeting from more than 35% of the votes *cast* with regard to one or more directors; or

- security holder approval at a prior meeting, based on a majority of the votes *cast*, to activate the security holder nominating procedure for future meetings, where the activation proposal has been made by a security holder or group of security holders that has held for one year more than 1% of the company's securities entitled to vote on the proposal.

In addition, the SEC is considering a third triggering event relating to a company's failure to implement a proposal on any other matter by a security holder or group of security holders meeting the above criteria and that was approved by more than 50% of the votes cast.

Once triggered, the nominating procedure would remain in effect with respect to any annual meeting held during the following two years. During that time, a company would be required to include in its proxy materials the director nominee(s) of a security holder or group of security holders that:

- has beneficially owned for two years more than 5% of the company's securities eligible to vote for the election of directors and intends to continue to own the securities until the annual meeting; and

- is eligible to file and has filed a short-form beneficial owner-ship report as an institutional or passive investor (Schedule 13G) before making the nomination.

The nominating security holder or group would be required to provide a notice with specified representations to the company, including representations that each director nominee meets eligibility standards, such as independence under applicable stock exchange listing standards and the absence of specified relationships with the nominating security holder.

References

SEC Rules

Reg. S-K Item 401(j)

Schedule 14A Item 7(d)

Proposed Rule 14a-11

SEC, NYSE & Nasdaq Websites (rules and commentary)

www.sec.gov/rules/sro/34-48745.htm

www.sec.gov/rules/final/33-8340.htm

www.sec.gov/rules/proposed/34-48626.htm

www.nyse.com/pdfs/finalcorpgovrules.pdf

www.nyse.com/pdfs/section303Afaqs.pdf

www.nasdaq.com/about/CorporateGovernance.pdf

COMPLIANCE CHECKLIST:
Bright-Line NYSE and Nasdaq Independence Tests
for Board of Directors of U.S. Listed Company

Requirement	NYSE	Nasdaq
Permitted director employment at listed company	Not executive officer	Not employee
Permitted direct compensation from listed company	$100,000 per year	$60,000 per year
Permitted payments between listed company and company where director is executive officer	2% of annual revenues of director's company (or $ 1 million, if greater)	5% of recipient's annual revenues (or $ 200,000, if greater)
Permitted payments between listed company and charity where director is executive officer	No limit—only triggers proxy statement disclosure	Same as payments to a director's company—see answer in previous row
Permitted compensation committee interlock—director is executive officer of company where listed company executive is on compensation committee	Not permitted	Not permitted

COMPLIANCE CHECKLIST:
Bright-Line NYSE and Nasdaq Independence Tests for Board of Directors of U.S. Listed Company

Requirement	NYSE	Nasdaq
Permitted director relationship with internal or external auditor of listed company	No employment with present or former internal or external auditor	Not present or former partner of external auditor (whether or not involved in the audit); not present or former employee of external auditor who worked on the audit
Application of above restrictions to immediate family members	Same, except employment by external auditor is considered only if in professional capacity	Same, except employment by listed company is considered only if executive officer
Look-back period	Three years	Three years
Transition period for look-back	Until Nov. 4, 2004, look-back is only one year.	No transition

Chapter 8

Governance: Audit Committee

Overview

An SEC rule mandated by the Sarbanes-Oxley Act and implemented through the U.S. stock exchanges requires heightened independence of audit committee members and strengthens the authority and responsibilities of the audit committees for listed companies. In their implementation, the stock exchanges have gone beyond the requirements of the SEC rule in some respects.

SEC Audit Committee Requirements

Companies Covered

With limited exceptions, the SEC audit committee rules apply to all U.S. and non-U.S. public companies with equity or debt listed on U.S. stock exchanges, including Nasdaq. Unlike the other stock exchange governance rules, there is no general exception for non-U.S. public companies with respect to these SEC audit committee requirements.

SEC Audit Committee Independence

The SEC requires each audit committee member to be independent under a standard that is generally stricter than the stock exchange director independence standards. However, unlike the NYSE and Nasdaq director independence standards discussed in chapter 7, the SEC audit committee independence rules cover only existing relationships and do not have a "look-back" test for prior relationships. Audit committee members must satisfy independence requirements of *both* the SEC and the stock exchange. Under the SEC rule, audit committee independence requires two things: absence of company compensation and non-affiliation, which are discussed below.

Prohibition on Compensatory Fees from the Company

In order to be independent, an audit committee member cannot accept, *directly or indirectly,* any consulting, advisory or other compensatory fee from the listed company or a subsidiary of the listed company, except in his or her capacity as a director or committee member.

If a committee member is a partner or executive officer or has a similar position in a law firm, accounting firm, consulting firm or investment bank that receives compensation from the listed company or any of its subsidiaries for services, he or she will not be considered independent. There is no *de minimis* exception; even a small amount of compensation will disqualify the committee member. In addition, indirect acceptance of a compensatory fee includes fees accepted by an audit committee member's immediate family members.

Affiliated Person

In order to be independent, an audit committee member cannot be an "affiliated person" of the listed company or a subsidiary of the listed company. That is, he or she cannot control, be controlled by or be under common control with the company or any subsidiary. A committee member is presumed not to be an affiliated person of an entity if he or she beneficially owns 10% or less of any class of its voting securities and does not serve as one of its executive officers.

Limited Exemptions from Independence Requirements

A company conducting its initial public offering must have one member of its audit committee independent at the time of listing. A majority of the members must be independent within ninety days and all members must be independent within one year.

Audit committee members may serve both on the audit committee of a listed company and on the audit committee of an affiliate of the company, so long as each member meets the independence requirements with respect to both companies.

There are special accommodations for non-U.S. listed companies that have employee board representation under home country requirements.

SEC Audit Committee Authority and Responsibilities

The SEC requires that the audit committee:

- select and oversee the outside auditors;
- establish whistleblower complaint procedures for accounting problems;
- be authorized to hire outside advisors; and
- be adequately funded by the company.

Selection and Oversight of Outside Auditors

The audit committee must be directly responsible for the appointment, compensation and oversight of the listed company's outside auditors, including resolving disagreements between management and the auditor regarding financial reporting. The SEC has indicated that the audit committee's oversight responsibility extends to the approval of all audit engagement fees and terms. The outside auditor is to report directly to the audit committee and the audit committee must pre-approve all services, audit and non-audit, provided by the outside auditor.

Complaint Procedures

The audit committee must establish procedures for the receipt, retention and treatment of complaints received by the listed company regarding accounting, internal accounting controls or auditing matters. These must include procedures for the confidential, anonymous submission by employees of concerns regarding questionable accounting or auditing matters.

Authority to Engage Advisors

The audit committee must have the authority to engage independent counsel and other advisors, as it determines necessary to carry out its duties.

Adequate Funding

Each listed company must provide the audit committee with appropriate funding, as determined by the committee. In addition to payment of compensation to the outside auditors, funding must cover any advisors employed by the audit committee and ordinary administrative expenses of the audit committee.

Selection and Oversight of Accounting Firms Other Than the Outside Auditors

The SEC staff has interpreted the SEC rules to require that the audit committee be directly responsible for pre-approving the appointment and compensation and for oversight of any other accounting firm that performs audit, review or attest services for the listed company. Unlike for the outside auditors, there is no requirement to pre-approve non-audit services provided by other accounting firms.

Disclosure Requirements

The SEC rules also require listed companies to disclose in their annual reports and proxy statements more information than in the past regarding their audit committee composition, independence and any exemption from independence being utilized.

SEC Audit Committee Financial Expert Disclosure

Required Disclosure

The SEC requires all U.S. and non-U.S. public companies to disclose in their annual reports whether or not they have at least one audit committee financial expert. This requirement applies even to non-listed public companies.

If a company has an audit committee financial expert, it must disclose the person's name and whether that person is independent under the applicable U.S. listing standards, even if the company is not listed. If the company has more than one audit committee financial expert, disclosure about the others is optional, but most companies will probably disclose as many as they have. There is no requirement to have an audit committee financial expert, but if the company does not have one, it must disclose why it does not.

Definition of Audit Committee Financial Expert

An audit committee financial expert must have all the following five attributes, as determined by the company's board of directors:

- an understanding of generally accepted accounting principles and financial statements;

- the ability to assess the general application of those accounting principles in connection with the accounting for estimates, accruals and reserves;

- experience preparing, auditing, analyzing or evaluating financial statements that present a breadth and level of complexity of accounting issues that are generally comparable to the breadth and complexity of companies that can reasonably be expected to be raised by the company's financial statements, or experience actively supervising these activities;

- an understanding of internal controls and procedures for financial reporting; and

- an understanding of audit committee functions.

A person must have acquired the five required attributes through one or more of the following means:

- education and experience as a principal financial officer, principal accounting officer, controller, public accountant or auditor, or positions that involve similar functions;

- experience actively supervising a person performing the above functions;

- experience overseeing or assessing the performance of companies or public accountants with respect to the preparation, auditing or evaluation of financial statements; or

- other relevant experience.

The SEC has stated that mere designation of a person as an audit committee financial expert will not impose any duties, obligations or liability on that person that are greater than those imposed on members of the audit committee and board of directors who do not carry this designation.

Additional NYSE Requirements

NYSE Independence and Other Qualifications

In addition to the SEC audit committee rules discussed above, the NYSE requires that audit committee members of a NYSE-listed company meet the general NYSE director independence requirements discussed in chapter 7.

The audit committee must consist of at least three members, all of whom are "financially literate." At least one must have "accounting or related financial management expertise," which is presumed to be the case for an "audit committee financial expert" under the SEC rule discussed on page 92.

If an audit committee member serves on the audit committees of more than two other public companies (in other words, three or more in total), the listed company must disclose that fact in its annual proxy statement as well as that its board has determined that the simultaneous service would not impair the ability of the director to serve on the listed company's audit committee.

NYSE Audit Committee Authority and Responsibilities

The NYSE requires the audit committee to have the following responsibilities, in addition to those required by the SEC:

- obtain at least annually a report from the outside auditors;

- discuss the annual audited financial statements and quarterly financial statements with management and the outside auditors;

- review and discuss earnings press releases, and financial information and earnings guidance provided to analysts and rating agencies;

- discuss policies with respect to risk assessment and risk management;

- meet separately, periodically, with management, the company's internal auditors and the outside auditors;

- review with the outside auditors any audit problems or difficulties and management's response;

- review specified information in connection with the company's financial statements and disclosure;

- set clear hiring policies for employees or former employees of the outside auditors;

- report regularly to the board of directors; and

- perform an annual performance self-evaluation.

The audit committee must also adopt a written charter that is posted on the company's website.

Additional Nasdaq Requirements

Nasdaq Independence and Other Qualifications

In addition to the SEC audit committee rules discussed above, Nasdaq requires that audit committee members of a Nasdaq-listed company meet the general Nasdaq director independence requirements discussed in chapter 7, including the look-back provisions.

The audit committee must consist of at least three members, all of whom must be able to read and understand fundamental financial statements. At least one must have past employment experience in finance or accounting, a professional certification in accounting, or comparable financial sophistication. A member who satisfies the SEC definition of "audit committee financial expert" discussed on page 92 is presumed to qualify as financially sophisticated.

Under exceptional and limited circumstances, one committee member may be non-independent but must nevertheless not be a company employee and may not serve more than two years.

Nasdaq Audit Committee Authority and Responsibilities

In addition to the responsibilities assigned by the SEC, Nasdaq requires the audit committee to oversee the company's accounting and financial reporting processes and the audits of its financial statements.

Nasdaq requires that each listed company have a written audit committee charter and that the audit committee have reviewed and reassessed the adequacy of the charter on an annual basis.

Approval of Related Party Transactions

Nasdaq also requires that each listed company's audit committee, or another independent board committee, approve all transactions between the company and its officers and directors that would be required to be disclosed under the SEC rule governing proxy statement disclosure of management transactions and other related party transactions. The NYSE does not have such a requirement.

Required Auditor Communications with Audit Committee

Auditor communications with the audit committee required under the SOA are discussed in chapter 11 on page 130.

References

Sarbanes-Oxley Act

§§ 204, 301 & 407

SEC Rules

Rule 10A-3 & Reg. S-K Items 401(h) & (i)

SEC Website (rules and commentary)

www.sec.gov/rules/final/33-8220.htm

www.sec.gov/rules/final/33-8177.htm

www.sec.gov/rules/sro/34-48745.htm

COMPLIANCE CHECKLIST:
Audit Committee of the Board of Directors

	Listed Companies[1]		Unlisted Public Companies[2]
	U.S.	Non-U.S.[3]	
Qualifications for Committee Members			
Must meet SEC strict independence test while on committee	✓	✓	
Must meet stock exchange independence test looking back three years	✓		
Must be financially literate/able to read basic financial statements	✓		
Must disclose name of one audit committee financial expert, or else why there is not one	✓	✓	✓
One member must have accounting expertise/financial sophistication (satisfied by being financial expert)	✓		
Must have at least three members	✓		
May serve on more than three public company audit committees only if board determines simultaneous service will not impair ability to serve (only NYSE-listed companies)	✓		
Committee Meetings			
At least quarterly; in practice more often	✓		
Periodically, meet separately with management, internal auditors and external auditors (only NYSE-listed companies)	✓		

COMPLIANCE CHECKLIST:
Audit Committee of the Board of Directors

Duties of Committee	Listed Companies[1] U.S.	Listed Companies[1] Non-U.S.[3]	Unlisted Public Companies[2]
Select and oversee external auditor	✓	✓	
Pre-approve all audit and non-audit services furnished by external auditor	✓	✓	✓
Generally oversee financial reporting process	✓		
Approve all audit and attest services furnished by external accounting firm that is not the external auditor of the SEC-filed financial statements	✓	✓	
Prepare audit committee report for annual proxy statement (only U.S. companies)	✓		✓
Receive reports from management about any internal control deficiencies—quarterly for U.S. companies, annually for non-U.S.	✓	✓	✓
Receive reports from external auditor annually about critical accounting policies, alternative accounting treatments, other material written communications to management	✓	✓	✓
Receive up-the-ladder reports from attorneys about material violations	✓	✓	✓
Establish procedures for anonymous whistleblower complaints about accounting	✓	✓	
Access to sufficient funding and to outside advisors	✓	✓	

COMPLIANCE CHECKLIST:
Audit Committee of the Board of Directors

Listed Companies[1]		Unlisted Public Companies[2]	
U.S.	Non-U.S.[3]		
✓			Adopt written charter and post on company website (only NYSE-listed companies must post)
✓			Additional duties (only NYSE-listed companies): • obtain report from external auditor annually regarding audit quality and independence matters; • discuss annual and quarterly financials with management and external auditor; • review quarterly earnings releases, earnings guidance, etc.; • discuss risk policies; • review audit problems with external auditor; • review specified information regarding financial disclosure; • set hiring policies for employees of external auditor; • report regularly to board of directors; and • perform annual self-evaluation.

[1] Listed on NYSE, Nasdaq or Amex.
[2] These are U.S. or non-U.S. companies that are required to file SEC reports, such as 10-K, 20-F or 40-F, but are not listed on a U.S. stock exchange.
[3] If not checked, non-U.S. companies are either exempt from the requirement (NYSE) or may seek an exemption (Nasdaq and Amex).

COMPLIANCE CHECKLIST:
Audit Committee Financial Expert

Required Attributes

Understanding of generally accepted accounting principles

Ability to assess accounting for estimates, accruals and reserves

One of the following:[1]

> Experience preparing, auditing, analyzing or evaluating comparable financial statements

> Experience actively supervising the above

Understanding of internal controls

Understanding of audit committee functions

Required Experience

Chief financial or accounting officer, controller

Certified public accountant

Auditor

Active supervision of the above

Financial analyst or other experience evaluating financial statements

Regulator of public companies regarding financial statements

Regulator of auditors regarding auditing

Other relevant experience—must be specifically described in annual proxy statement

---

[1] Although somewhat redundant, the SEC rule requires, as one of the five required attributes, first-hand experience or active supervision in preparing, auditing, analyzing or evaluating financial statements, even though there is also a specific requirement to have experience in essentially the same areas, as described under "Required Experience."

Chapter 9

Other Director Governance Matters

Codes of Ethics

SEC Code of Ethics Requirement

Required Disclosure

The SEC requires each U.S. and non-U.S. public company to disclose in its SEC annual report whether it has adopted a written code of ethics that applies to its senior financial officers, including its principal executive officer, principal financial officer, principal accounting officer or controller, or persons performing similar functions. This requirement applies whether or not the company is listed.

A company is not required by the SEC to have a code of ethics, but if it does not, the company must disclose why it has not adopted one. As discussed in the sections "NYSE Code of Ethics Requirement" and "Nasdaq Code of Conduct Requirement," on page 103, the stock exchanges do require their listed companies to adopt codes of ethics and to apply the codes to directors and all employees. A listed company may adopt a single code satisfying both SEC and stock exchange requirements.

Scope of the Code of Ethics

To qualify as a code of ethics under the SEC rule, the code must be reasonably designed to deter wrongdoing and to promote:

- honest and ethical conduct;
- full, fair, accurate, timely and understandable disclosure to the public;
- compliance with applicable governmental laws, rules and regulations;
- prompt internal reporting of violations of the code; and
- accountability for adherence to the code.

Public Availability

If a company has a code of ethics, it must make available to the public a copy of the code or the relevant portions by:

- filing a copy with its SEC annual report;
- posting the code on its Internet website and disclosing the

website address in its annual report; or

- stating in its annual report that it will provide without charge a copy of the code.

Amendments and Waivers

Any substantive amendment to the code of ethics or waiver from any provision must be publicly disclosed if it applies to a senior financial officer.

U.S. public companies may choose to disclose an amendment or waiver either by filing a report on Form 8-K with the SEC or by posting a website notice. In either case, U.S. companies must make the disclosure within four business days. Non-U.S. public companies are required to disclose amendments and waivers of the code of ethics only on an annual basis in their annual reports, although more prompt disclosure, such as by filing a report on Form 6-K or website posting, is encouraged by the SEC.

NYSE Code of Ethics Requirement

The NYSE requires that each NYSE-listed U.S. company adopt a code of business conduct and ethics covering all of its directors, officers and employees, not merely senior financial officers. The code must be posted on the company's website. It must address a more specific list of situations than the SEC code, including avoiding conflicts of interest, protecting corporate opportunities, maintaining confidentiality of corporate information and protecting company assets.

Any waiver of the code for executive officers or directors may be made only by the board of directors or a board committee and must be promptly disclosed to shareholders, such as by issuing a press release, making a website posting or submitting a report on Form 8-K.

Non-U.S. listed companies are exempt from these additional NYSE requirements if they so disclose, as discussed in chapter 7 on page 75.

Nasdaq Code of Conduct Requirement

Nasdaq also requires Nasdaq-listed companies to have a code of conduct applicable to all directors, officers and employees, not merely senior financial officers. Nasdaq does not specify situations that the code must cover beyond those specified for the SEC code.

Any waiver from the code for executive officers or directors must be approved by the board of directors. U.S. public companies must disclose waivers in a report on Form 8-K filed within four business days. Website posting is not an alternative for Nasdaq-listed companies. Non-U.S. listed companies have the option of disclosing waivers either in a report on Form 6-K or in their next annual report on Form 20-F, unless they have obtained an exemption from Nasdaq as discussed in chapter 7 on page 77.

Shareholder Approval of Equity Compensation Plans

The NYSE, Nasdaq and Amex each require shareholder approval of equity compensation plans. While the rules are generally similar, they differ in specifics. The NYSE and Nasdaq requirements are described below. The Amex requirements are generally the same as those of Nasdaq.

NYSE Rule on Shareholder Approval of Equity Compensation Plans

The NYSE requires a listed U.S. company to obtain shareholder approval of all equity compensation plans and all material revisions to these plans. Also, whether or not the company itself is listed on the NYSE, in voting on equity plans on behalf of customers holding in "street names," NYSE member brokers must obtain specific voting instructions from their customers and may not use general discretionary voting authority that applies to routine non-contested matters.

The NYSE shareholder approval requirement covers any plan or other arrangement that provides for the delivery of equity securities, whether newly issued or treasury securities, of the listed company to any employee, director or other service provider as compensation for services. There are special rules for plans known as "formula plans" and "discretionary plans."

In addition, the NYSE rules provide three categories of exemptions from the shareholder approval requirement:

- employment inducement awards;
- plans acquired in mergers and acquisitions; and
- tax-qualified plans and so-called "parallel excess plans."

Grants and plans relying on these exemptions still require approval by the company's compensation committee or independent directors, and notification to the NYSE. Non-U.S. companies are exempt from the NYSE requirement to obtain shareholder approval of equity plans.

Nasdaq Rule on Shareholder Approval of Equity Compensation Plans

Nasdaq requires listed companies to obtain shareholder approval to establish or materially amend a stock option or purchase plan or to make any other arrangement under which options or stock may be acquired by officers, directors, employees or consultants. The rule also has special requirements for so-called "formula plans" and "open-end plans." Non-U.S. companies may obtain exemptions as discussed in chapter 7, on page 77.

Under the Nasdaq rule, the following are exempted from the shareholder approval requirement:

- generally available plans;
- employment inducement awards;
- tax-qualified plans and parallel non-qualified plans;
- convenience plans; and
- plans relating to an acquisition or merger.

Disclosure of Equity Compensation Plan Information

The SEC requires U.S. public companies to make disclosure about equity compensation plans not approved by shareholders and requires copies of the plans to be filed with the company's annual report or proxy statement. The SEC disclosures apply even to non-listed U.S. public companies. The disclosures do not apply to non-U.S. companies.

Other NYSE Corporate Governance Rules

NYSE CEO Certification and Notice of Noncompliance

The NYSE requires CEOs of listed companies to certify annually to the NYSE as to their company's compliance with the NYSE corporate governance listing standards.

Furthermore, the NYSE requires CEOs of listed companies to notify the NYSE promptly after any executive officer of the company becomes aware of any material noncompliance with any of the NYSE corporate governance standards. Under SEC rules, any such notice must be publicly disclosed on Form 8-K within four business days.

The NYSE rules require that the annual CEO/CFO "civil" certification filed with the SEC also be included in the company's annual report sent to shareholders. The SEC's CEO/CFO certification is discussed in chapter 2.

NYSE Public Reprimand Letters

The NYSE now has the authority to issue public reprimand letters to listed companies that violate any NYSE listing standard, including corporate governance standards. The NYSE continues to have the authority also to commence delisting proceedings. A public reprimand letter or delisting also requires prompt public Form 8-K disclosure by the company.

Other Nasdaq Corporate Governance Rules

Nasdaq Notice of Noncompliance

Nasdaq, like the NYSE, requires a listed company promptly to notify Nasdaq after an executive officer of the company becomes aware of any material noncompliance with any of Nasdaq's corporate governance standards. Any such notice must be publicly disclosed on Form

8-K filed with the SEC within four business days. Unlike the NYSE, Nasdaq does not require an annual certification.

Nasdaq Disclosure of Going Concern Qualifications

Under the Nasdaq rules, a listed company receiving an audit opinion that expresses substantial doubt about the company's ability to continue as a going concern must make a public announcement disclosing the receipt of this qualification within seven days after the audit opinion is included in an SEC filing.

References

Sarbanes-Oxley Act

§ 406

SEC Rules

Reg. S-K Items 201(d) & 406

SEC, NYSE & Nasdaq Websites (rules and commentary)

www.sec.gov/rules/final/33-8177.htm

www.sec.gov/rules/sro/34-48108.htm

www.sec.gov/rules/sro/34-48627.htm

www.sec.gov/rules/sro/34-48745.htm

www.nyse.com/pdfs/section303Afaqs.pdf

www.nyse.com/pdfs/equitycompfaqs.pdf

www.nasdaq.com/about/CorporateGovernance.pdf

COMPLIANCE CHECKLIST:
SEC, NYSE and Nasdaq Code of Ethics Requirements

	SEC	NYSE	Nasdaq
Nature of Requirement	Disclosure requirement only Not required to adopt a code, but must disclose why not if no code	Must adopt a code	Must adopt a code
Companies Subject to Requirement	US and non-U.S. public companies	NYSE-listed U.S. companies	Nasdaq-listed companies Non-US listed companies may seek an exemption
Covered Persons	Senior financial officers	All directors, officers and employees	All directors, officers and employees
Scope of Code	Must be reasonably designed to deter wrong-doing and promote: • Honest and ethical conduct; • Full, fair, accurate, timely and understandable disclosure to the public; • Compliance with laws; • Prompt internal reporting of code violations; and • Accountability for adherence to code.	Must also cover specified areas beyond those for the SEC code, including: • Avoiding conflicts of interest; • Protecting corporate opportunities; • Maintaining confidentiality of corporate information; and • Protecting company assets.	Only required to cover areas specified for the SEC code

COMPLIANCE CHECKLIST:
SEC, NYSE and Nasdaq Code of Ethics Requirements

	SEC	NYSE	Nasdaq
Disclosure of Code	File a copy with SEC annual report; *or* Post on company website; *or* State in annual report that company will provide copies without charge.	Must post on company website	Must be publicly available
Amendments/ Waivers	Amendments and waivers must be publicly disclosed: <ul><li>by submitting an 8-K report or website posting for U.S. public companies; or</li><li>in annual reports for non-U.S. public companies.</li></ul>	Waivers for executive officers or directors must be approved by board or board committee. Must also be promptly disclosed to shareholders, such as by <ul><li>issuing a press release, *or*</li><li>website posting, *or*</li><li>submitting an 8-K report.</li></ul>	Waivers for executive officers or directors must be approved by board or board committee. Must also be disclosed in an 8-K report (6-K or next annual report for non-U.S. listed companies).

Chapter 10

Governance: Executive Officers and Directors

Overview

To address perceived governance problems involving "insiders" of public companies in the wake of the corporate financial scandals, the Sarbanes-Oxley Act imposed tightened requirements on executive officers and directors of public companies. These include:

- shorter deadlines for public insider share transaction reports;

- a prohibition on loans to insiders;

- a blackout on insider share transactions during 401(k) and similar benefit plan trading blackouts;

- CEO and CFO bonus disgorgement in the event of financial restatement;

- a prohibition on improperly influencing audits; and

- SEC authority to freeze payments to insiders during investigations.

Shorter Deadlines for Ownership Reports by Insiders of U.S. Public Companies

Federal securities laws require each executive officer and director of a U.S. public company to report publicly his or her beneficial ownership of all equity securities of the company and changes in his or her ownership, by filing Forms 3, 4 and 5 with the SEC. Beneficial owners of more than 10% of the common stock of a U.S. public company and of certain other classes of equity must also file these reports.

Shorter Deadlines

The SOA changed these so-called "Section 16 reports" to:

- shorten the filing deadline for Form 4 reports of changes of beneficial ownership to two business days following the execution of the transaction; ownership changes were previously reportable monthly within ten days after the end of the month in which the transaction occurred;

- require reporting on Form 4, within two business days of the transaction, of all grants, awards and other purchases of equity securities from the company, sales to the company and discretionary transactions where the director or officer can select the date of execution; these transactions with the company were previously reportable annually on a deferred basis on Form 5 within forty-five days after the end of the company's fiscal year;

- permit up to three extra business days for reporting transactions pursuant to some plans and arrangements where the insider does not select the execution date, as these transactions cannot feasibly be reported within two business days; and

- eliminate the deferred reporting exception for small acquisitions (up to $10,000 in market value) from the company or an employee benefit plan, instead requiring these to be reported on Form 4 within two business days.

Mandatory Electronic Filing and Website Posting

The SOA also mandated electronic filing and website posting of reports on Forms 3, 4 and 5. The SEC established a web-based filing system, available at <https://www.onlineforms.edgarfiling.sec.gov>, as the exclusive means of filing these forms. The forms may be filed electronically between 8:00 A.M. and 10:00 P.M., Washington, D.C. time, on SEC business days.

The SEC rules also require a company that maintains a corporate website to post these forms on its website by the end of the business day after filing and to keep them accessible for at least a twelve-month period. Companies may satisfy this requirement by using hyperlinks to the SEC's website that meet the SEC's criteria.

Prohibition on Loans to Officers and Directors

The SOA prohibits U.S. and non-U.S. public companies from making or arranging personal loans to their executive officers and directors. There are no general SEC clarifying regulations.

The SOA exempts loans maintained by a company before July 30, 2002, so long as there is no material modification to any term of the loan or any renewal of the loan. The SOA also exempts consumer credit, margin loans and certain other types of loans by U.S. banks to executive officers and directors of the public parent or other affiliate of the lender, so long as these loans are:

- provided in the ordinary course of the lender's consumer credit business;
- of a type the lender generally makes available to the public; and
- on market terms the lender offers to the general public.

In addition, the SEC exempted qualified foreign banks and their parent or affiliates from the SOA prohibition on loans to executive officers and directors if the above criteria are met.

Although each situation should be analyzed individually, the following are considered by many as still permissible and not covered by the SOA prohibition on loans to executive officers and directors:

- indemnification advances to executive officers or directors;
- bona fide travel advances and issuance of company credit cards that are used primarily for ordinary company business and are repaid promptly in accordance with reasonable business practices;
- personal use of a company car, whether or not reimbursement is required;
- loans from 401(k) plans; and
- cashless option exercises.

Benefit Plan Blackouts

Prohibited Insider Trades During a Blackout Period

Executive officers and directors of U.S. and non-U.S. public companies are prohibited by the SEC from trading in the company's common stock or other equity securities during a benefit plan "blackout" period. The prohibition applies to all stock or other equity they acquired in connection with service or employment as a director or executive officer of the company but not to pre-existing ownership.

This part of the SOA is among those traceable to the Enron situation, in which the CEO sold shares as the stock plummeted while the rank-and-file was blacked out for weeks from switching out of the company stock fund in the 401(k) plan while a change of plan administrators was taking place.

A blackout period arises if 50% or more of the U.S. participants in the company's defined contribution plans, such as 401(k) plans and employee stock ownership plans, are suspended from purchasing, selling or transferring company stock or other equity for a period of more than three consecutive business days. However, it does not include:

- regularly scheduled blackout periods that are part of the plan; and

- blackouts imposed to consolidate plans as a result of a merger or similar corporate transaction involving the company.

The prohibition applies to a non-U.S. public company only if more than 15% of its worldwide employees are U.S. persons who would be blacked out or if more than 50,000 U.S. participants would be blacked out.

Department of Labor Advance Notice Rule

The U.S. Department of Labor, which regulates employee benefit plans, requires plan administrators to give participants thirty days' advance written notice of a plan blackout period. Notice must also be provided to the company so it can give the required notice to insiders and the SEC, as described below.

Notice of a Blackout Period to Insiders and the SEC

A public company must provide notice of a blackout period to its executive officers and directors within five business days after the company receives the notice from the plan administrator. Even if the company does not receive a notice from the plan administrator, the company must notify executive officers and directors at least fifteen calendar days before the actual or expected beginning date of the blackout period.

In addition, a company must provide notice of a blackout period to the SEC. For U.S. public companies, the SEC notice must be filed on Form 8-K on the same day notice is transmitted to executive officers and directors. Non-U.S. public companies must file the notice as an exhibit to their annual report on Form 20-F or 40-F.

Disgorgement for Restatements

Under the SOA, CEO and CFO disgorgement is required if a public company is required to prepare an accounting restatement due to material noncompliance, as a result of misconduct, with financial reporting requirements. In that event, the CEO and CFO of the company must reimburse the company for any bonus or other incentive-based compensation or equity-based compensation during the twelve-month period following initial publication of the financial statements that had to be restated. They must also pay to the company any profits from their sale of the company's securities during that period.

This is a relatively untested provision, and there are no clarifying SEC rules. Accordingly, there remain questions about how this part of the law operates, including what is meant by "misconduct" and whether misconduct by persons other than the CEO and CFO is relevant.

Improper Influence on Conduct of Audits

Officers and directors of a U.S. or non-U.S. public company are expressly prohibited from directly or indirectly exerting improper influence on the conduct of an audit or review of financial statements. The prohibition covers any action taken to coerce, manipulate, mislead or fraudulently influence any independent accountant engaged in auditing or reviewing the SEC financial statements of the company, if these persons knew or should have known that the action, if successful, could render the company's financial statements materially misleading.

SEC Temporary Freeze on Bonus and Special Payments

The SEC has authority under the SOA to seek a court order to temporarily freeze any "extraordinary payments" proposed to be made by a U.S. or non-U.S. public company to any of its directors, officers and some affiliated parties during the course of an investigation of the company for possible securities law violations.

References

Sarbanes-Oxley Act

§§ 303, 304, 306, 402, 403(a) & 1103

SEC Rules

Rule 16a-3, Rule 13k-1, Reg. BTR & Rule 13b2-2

SEC & Department of Labor Websites
(rules and commentary)

www.sec.gov/rules/final/34-46421.htm

www.sec.gov/rules/final/33-8230.htm

www.sec.gov/rules/final/34-47225.htm

www.dol.gov/ebsa/regs/fedreg/final/2003001430.pdf

Chapter 11

Auditor Independence and Safeguards Against Auditor Conflicts

Overview

SEC rules regulating auditor independence were overhauled in 2001. The SOA made them stricter, starting in 2003, but did not make fundamental changes. For example, many types of non-audit services were already prohibited by the 2001 rules. However, the SOA heightened sensitivities to the auditor independence rules by requiring audit committee pre-approval of all audit and non-audit engagements. This chapter describes all the auditor independence rules.

General Auditor Independence Principles

The touchstone of the SEC's auditor independence rules is the integrity of financial statements and the resultant investor confidence in those financial statements. The SEC has stated: "It is the auditor's opinion that furnishes investors with critical assurance that the financial statements have been subjected to a rigorous examination by an objective, impartial and skilled professional, and that investors, therefore, can rely on them."

The SEC independence rules set forth the general standard of independence: an accountant's independence is impaired if a reasonable investor with knowledge of all relevant facts and circumstances would conclude that the accountant is not capable of exercising objective and impartial judgment on all issues encompassed within the accountant's judgment. The rules describe four factors the SEC considers in evaluating auditor independence questions:

- whether there is a mutual or conflicting interest between the accountant and the audit client;

- whether the accountant is in the position of auditing his or her own work;

- whether the accountant acts as management or an employee of the audit client; and

- whether the accountant is in a position of being an advocate for the audit client.

The SEC independence rules also set forth a list of circumstances implementing the general principles that automatically result in impaired auditor independence. Situations not covered by the list must still be tested under the general independence principles noted above. This list, as modified by the SOA, covers:

- prohibited non-audit services;

- required audit committee pre-approval of engagements of the accountant;

- independence-impairing financial, business and payment relationships with the audit client;

- audit partner rotation;

- independence-impairing employment relationships between the accountant and the audit client; and

- prohibition on audit partner compensation for cross-selling non-audit services.

The SOA also added some other safeguards against auditor conflicts, also described in this chapter, such as an express prohibition on improper influence by companies of their auditors.

The auditor independence rules apply equally to U.S. and non-U.S. public companies.

Evolution of Current Independence Rules

In 2001, the SEC implemented a major overhaul of its auditor independence rules. The revised rules addressed many areas with much greater specificity than before and reflected a general tightening of the requirements. The revisions, which generally became effective on February 5, 2001, had engendered some controversy when proposed as being too strict.

The 2001 revisions tightened the prohibitions on security ownership and other financial interests by audit professionals in audit clients and established a list of prohibited services, including substantially limiting the amount of financial information systems consulting that audit firms were permitted to perform for audit clients. The rules also prohibited business and employment relationships with audit clients and contingent fees and required former audit professionals to sever financial and other ties with the accounting firm when becoming employed by an audit client. The rule revisions reflected compromises resulting from discussions between the Big Five accounting firms and the SEC following the initial proposal in early 2000.

In 2002, the SOA tightened the rules in a few respects. Contrary to popular belief, the SOA made no major changes, as the rules were already quite strict as a result of the 2001 revisions. The SOA eliminated many of the exceptions to the list of prohibited non-audit services in the 2001 independence rules and added "expert services" as a new category of prohibited service. Another change—and perhaps the one with the highest profile—was to require audit committee pre-approval of all services performed by the accounting firm. As a result, many audit committee members and inside and outside legal advisors were for the first time required to consider issues arising under the auditor independence rules.

The SOA also required audit partner rotation and a one-year cooling-off period before audit engagement team members may accept employment at an audit client. In implementing these new requirements, which generally became effective on May 6, 2003, the SEC also added a prohibition, not required by the SOA, on the accounting firm's compensating audit partners for cross-selling non-audit services.

Thus, while the SOA expanded the scope of the auditor independence rules, many of the requirements have been in effect since early 2001. Prior to the SOA, issuers may have been more inclined to defer to their accounting firms for compliance with those rules. Given the new audit committee pre-approval requirements and the generally greater focus on governance and financial reporting matters following enactment of the SOA, issuers and their inside and external counsel are becoming increasingly involved in matters of auditor independence.

Prohibited Non-Audit Services

The prohibitions on specified non-audit services are, according to the SEC, "largely predicated" on three basic principles. In particular, an accountant cannot:

(1)   audit its own work;

(2)   function in the role of management; or

(3)   serve in an advocacy role for its client.

The enumerated prohibited non-audit services generally invoke one or more of those three concepts. Each category of prohibited services is described below.

Bookkeeping and Related Services

The rule prohibits *any* bookkeeping and related service, unless it is reasonable to conclude that the results will not be subject to audit procedures.

Financial Information Systems Design and Implementation

The rule prohibits services in which an accountant designs or implements a hardware or software system that aggregates source data underlying the financial statements or generates information that is significant to the audit client's other financial information systems taken as a whole. The 2003 revisions eliminated a previous exception permitting some of these services if management does not rely on the accountant's work as the primary basis for determining the adequacy of its internal controls and financial reporting systems.

Appraisal or Valuation Services, Fairness Opinions or Contribution-in-Kind Reports

An audit firm is prohibited from providing appraisal or valuation services or fairness opinions (called a contribution-in-kind report in some countries), unless it is reasonable to conclude the results will not be subject to audit procedures.

Actuarial Services

The rule prohibits *any* actuarially oriented advisory service involving the determination of amounts recorded in the financial statements and related accounts other than assisting a client in understanding the methods, models, assumptions and requests used in computing an amount, unless it is reasonable to conclude the results will not be subject to audit procedures.

Internal Audit Outsourcing

An audit firm is prohibited from providing any internal audit service that relates to internal accounting controls, financial systems or financial statements, unless it is reasonable to conclude the results will not be subject to audit procedures. Operational internal audits unrelated to accounting and financial matters are permitted.

Management Functions

An audit firm is not permitted to act, even temporarily, as a director, officer or *employee* of an audit client. The audit firm also must not perform any decision-making, supervisory or ongoing monitoring functions for the audit client.

Human Resources

Five human resources functions are prohibited—seeking candidates for managerial or director positions, testing or evaluation, reference checks, negotiating benefits or other terms and recommending the hiring of specific candidates.

Broker-Dealer, Investment Adviser and Investment Banking Services

The rule prohibits an audit firm from acting as broker-dealer (even if unregistered) or investment banker for an audit client, making investment decisions for the client or having custody of audit client assets.

Legal Services

The rule prohibits all services for which the service provider must be licensed, admitted or otherwise qualified to practice law in the relevant jurisdiction. The SEC has clarified that a service in a non-U.S. jurisdiction will not be a prohibited "legal service" if it may be performed by non-lawyers in the United States, even if it is a service provided by attorneys in the non-U.S. jurisdiction.

Expert Services

Under the prohibition on "expert services," a category added in the 2003 revisions, an audit firm may not provide an expert opinion or other expert service for the purpose of advocating an audit client's interests in litigation or in a regulatory or administrative proceeding or investigation. Whether or not a proceeding or regulatory investigation has commenced, the audit firm may not be engaged to work for the audit client's legal counsel.

Tax Services

An audit firm may provide tax compliance, tax planning and tax advice services to an audit client, but may not represent an audit client before a tax court, district court or federal court of claims. The

SEC has cautioned audit committees to "scrutinize carefully" the retention of an audit firm for tax services for a transaction initially recommended by the audit firm, if the sole business purpose of the transaction may be tax avoidance and the tax treatment of the transaction may not be supported.

Audit Committee Pre-Approval

The SEC adopted a rule in the 2003 revisions requiring audit committees to pre-approve all audit and non-audit services performed by the outside auditor. As an alternative to "direct" pre-approval by the audit committee, audit committees may develop pre-approval policies and procedures so long as:

- the policies and procedures are detailed as to the particular service;

- the audit committee is informed of each service; and

- the policies and procedures do not include delegation of the audit committee's approval responsibilities to management.

For example, an audit committee may adopt procedures describing services that are pre-approved and establishing fee caps on types of services and time limits within which the engagement must commence. The challenge is to describe the services, time limits and other criteria in sufficient detail and establish the fee limits at a sufficiently reasonable (that is, not too high) level to support the conclusion that the services have been pre-approved by the audit committee and there has been no delegation to management of approval responsibilities. Until there is further official guidance, audit committees will likely err on the side of greater particularity and more limited fee levels. Internal control-related services are specifically excluded from approval through the pre-approval procedures described in this paragraph.

In contrast to the above limitations, the audit committee is permitted to delegate all decision-making discretion to one or more audit committee members, as long as the decisions are reported at the next scheduled meeting of the full committee.

The rule also provides a *de minimis* exception, based on the statute, for failure to pre-approve permitted non-audit services if the services were not at first recognized to be non-audit services. The total fees for services under this exception must be 5% or less of annual audit fees, and the services must be approved by the audit committee during the same audit year.

Financial, Business and Payment Relationships

The independence rules also set forth a number of financial, business and payment relationships that would impair independence. Many of these rules are designed to protect against situations in which the auditor has an interest in the continued success of the audit client and as a result may be hesitant to perform rigorous audit procedures or present a qualified opinion on the audit client's financial statements.

The rules prohibit an auditor and certain related parties from investing or having other financial interests in audit clients, as well as direct business relationships (whether or not material) and material indirect business relationships. Other prohibited financial interests include loans to or from an audit client, savings and checking accounts with an audit client, broker-dealer or futures commission merchant accounts with an audit client, credit card balances owed to an audit client and insurance products issued by an audit client. The rules prohibit common investments with audit clients and investments by audit clients in the accounting firm. The rules also generally prohibit contingent fees.

Audit Partner Rotation

Lead and concurring audit partners are subject to a five-year rotation and a five-year time-out requirement. Other audit partners are required to rotate every seven years and observe a two-year time-out period.

Employment Relationships

The rule requires a one-year cooling-off period before an audit client may employ former members of the audit engagement team. The requirement applies to former partners, principals, shareholders or professional employees of an audit firm who seek employment in a "financial reporting oversight role" at an audit client.

Former partners, principals, shareholders and professional employees must also sever certain financial ties to the audit firm before they can become audit client employees, whether or not employed in a financial reporting oversight role. The rule also prohibits an audit client from employing a current auditor and certain relatives of the auditor.

Conversely, the rule prohibits the audit firm from employing former employees of the audit client in capacities where they could influence the audit of financial statements covering any period during which they were employed at the audit client.

Prohibition on Audit Partner Compensation for Cross-Selling Non-Audit Services

The rule prohibits any audit partner from receiving compensation based on the audit partner procuring engagements to provide products or services other than audit, review or attest services.

Enhanced Disclosure

In addition to modifying the rules relating to auditor independence, the SEC has enhanced the annual report and proxy statement disclosure requirements as they relate to services provided by outside auditors. Under these rules, public companies are required to disclose the fees paid to auditors for services in four categories for each of the past two fiscal years: audit, audit-related, tax and other. Companies must also disclose pre-approval policies and procedures adopted by the audit committee.

Consequences of Impaired Auditor Independence

The auditor independence rules are complex, are relatively strict, in many cases do not apply materiality thresholds and do not provide a means of retroactive cure for violations. Although a violation of many of these rules will impair independence and therefore have a direct impact on outside auditors (indeed, certain violations may constitute violations of the federal securities laws on the part of the auditor), a violation of the independence rules will impact public companies as well. A violation of the independence rules could result in a company's having to change auditors, make embarrassing public disclosures or arrange for supplemental audit work by another firm. A violation could also preclude the company from accessing the capital markets until remedial actions are completed. If the violation were sufficiently serious, a company could even be required to obtain a re-audit of the financial statements for the period affected by the independence impairment. Thus, audit committees considering independence issues can be expected to apply the rules conservatively.

In addition, it appears that the SEC is strictly interpreting its auditor independence rules and considers compliance by issuers and auditors a priority. For example, in April 2004, the SEC applied a broad range of civil sanctions against Ernst & Young's U.S. member firm for violations of the auditor independence rules in connection with its audits of PeopleSoft, Inc.'s financial statements for fiscal years 1994 through 1999. The sanctions included a six-month ban on Ernst & Young's U.S. member firm's taking on new public company audit clients.

Required Auditor Communications with the Audit Committee

Each registered public accounting firm is required to report the following to the audit committee before the audit report is filed with the SEC:

- all critical accounting policies and practices to be used;

- all alternative treatments within generally accepted accounting principles for policies and practices related to material items that have been discussed with management of the issuer, including:

  - ramifications of the use of such alternative disclosures and treatments, and

  - the treatment preferred by the registered public accounting firm; and

- other material written communications between the registered public accounting firm and the management of the issuer, such as any management letter or schedule of unadjusted differences.

Material Correcting Adjustments

The SOA elevated to a statutory mandate the previous requirement of generally accepted auditing standards that the financial statements must reflect material correcting adjustments identified by the auditors.

This provision does not appear to require substantive changes to the audit process.

In making a determination about the materiality of a proposed adjustment, consideration should be given to SEC Staff Accounting Bulletin No. 99, which notes that evaluation of materiality requires a company and its auditors to consider all of the relevant circumstances regarding the misstatement, rather than relying solely on a numerical or percentage-based threshold. Offsetting of two material misstatements is not permitted.

Retention of Audit Work Papers

U.S. and non-U.S. audit firms must retain for seven years most records relevant to their audits and reviews of financial statements of public companies. These records include workpapers and other records (including electronic records) that contain conclusions, opinions, analyses or financial data related to the audit or review. Audit firms must retain documents that are "inconsistent" with the final conclusions reached by the auditor, as well as those that support the conclusions.

Improper Influence on Conduct of Audits

An SEC rule prohibits officers and directors of a U.S. or non-U.S. public company from directly or indirectly exerting improper influence on the conduct of an audit or review of financial statements. The prohibition covers any action taken to coerce, manipulate, mislead or fraudulently influence any independent accountant engaged in auditing or reviewing the SEC financial statements if they knew or should have known that their actions, if successful, could result in rendering the company's financial statements materially misleading.

SEC Authority to Censure Accountants

The SOA confirms the SEC's statutory authority to censure or prohibit from appearing and practicing before the SEC any person found to be unqualified, to be lacking in integrity, to have engaged in "improper professional conduct," or to have willfully violated the securities laws. Improper professional conduct by an accountant encompasses a single instance of intentional, reckless or highly unreasonable conduct or repeated instances of unreasonable conduct.

References

Sarbanes-Oxley Act

§§ 201–04, 206, 303, 401(a), 602 & 802

SEC Rules

Reg. S-X Rules 2-01, 2-06 & 2-07

SEC Website (rules and commentary)

www.sec.gov/rules/final/33-7919.htm

www.sec.gov/rules/final/33-8183.htm

www.sec.gov/info/accountants/ocafaqaudind080703.htm

COMPLIANCE CHECKLIST:
Auditor Independence Requirements, Including Prohibited Services and Relationships

Prohibited non-audit services

Bookkeeping

Financial information systems design/implementation

Appraisal/valuation services and fairness opinions

Actuarial services

Internal audit outsourcing

Acting as director, officer or employee

Human resources

Broker-dealer, investment adviser and investment banking

Legal services

Expert services

Prohibited financial relationships

Applies to

Audit firm

Audit engagement team

Chain of command over audit team

Managerial employees performing significant non-audit services for audit client

Partners and principals in the same office as the audit partner

Spouses and dependents of above persons

Prohibited investments in audit clients

Direct investments (including trustee)

Over-5% equity investments—extends to any professional in the firm and also parents, children and siblings of covered persons

Material indirect investments

Some investments in intermediary investors that invest in the audit client

Some joint investments with the audit client

Prohibited financial interests in audit clients

Loans of any size—with a few exception categories

Savings and checking accounts with balances exceeding $100,000

Broker-dealer accounts with balances exceeding $500,000

Futures and commodities accounts

Credit card balances exceeding $10,000

Insurance policies—restriction applies only to individuals, not to audit firm itself

Mutual funds—where audit client is sponsor or adviser or a member of the family of funds

Prohibited business relationships with audit clients

Direct business relationship, regardless of size—excluding permitted professional services by the audit firm

Material indirect business relationship

Prohibited audit clients' financial relationships

Investment in the audit firm

Audit client acts as underwriter, promoter or similar for audit firm securities

Prohibited contingent fees

Audit firm receives a contingent fee, unless fee amount is fixed by court or regulator

Prohibited employment relationships

Former audit firm professional employees becoming employed at audit client

Sever all financial ties to audit firm, generally including cash-out of pension interests

One-year cooling-off period if position is director, chief executive or operating officer, president, chief financial or accounting officer, controller, treasurer, director of financial reporting or internal audit, general counsel or equivalent

Family member of audit firm professional employee becoming employed at audit client

Prohibited if

Audit firm professional is involved in the audit or supervising it;

Family member is in accounting or financial reporting oversight role at audit client; and

Family relationship is spouse, parent, child (whether or not dependent), dependent or sibling

Former audit client employee becoming employed at audit firm

Prohibited if

Position at audit firm involves influence on audit client's financial statements; and

Financial statements correspond to period of employment at audit client

Prohibited audit partner cross-selling

No audit partner compensation for procuring tax or other non-audit engagements

Required audit partner rotation

Lead and concurring audit partners—5-year rotation and 5-year time-out

Other audit partners—7-year rotation and 2-year time-out

Required audit committee pre-approval

Audit committee must pre-approve all services—audit and non-audit—performed by audit firm

Chapter 12

Public Company Accounting Oversight Board

Overview

The Sarbanes-Oxley Act overhauled the self-regulatory structure that had long existed in the accounting profession in the United States. It created the Public Company Accounting Oversight Board, or the PCAOB, an SEC-supervised regulatory body structured much like the National Association of Securities Dealers, Inc., which regulates broker-dealers.

All U.S. and non-U.S. public accounting firms that audit SEC-reporting public companies must register with the PCAOB, which has the authority to set auditing and related standards, conduct inspections and investigations of registered public accounting firms and impose a wide range of sanctions on these firms or their associated persons, in each case subject to the SEC's oversight. The establishment of accounting standards remains with the private sector not-for-profit Financial Accounting Standards Board.

This chapter discusses the PCAOB's four major duties and responsibilities under the SOA:

- auditor registration;
- audit standard-setting;
- inspections; and
- enforcement.

Auditor Registration

Each public accounting firm that issues an audit report with respect to a public company must be registered with the PCAOB. U.S. public accounting firms were required to register by October 22, 2003, and non-U.S. public accounting firms by July 19, 2004.

The Big Four and many other public accounting firms are organized as associations of accounting firms separately organized in each country but doing business under a common name and coordinated practice policies. Each country-specific firm must separately register with the PCAOB. In addition, any firm that plays a substantial role in the audit of a public company, such as through an audit of a significant subsidiary, must register with the PCAOB.

Auditing, Quality Control and Independence Standards

Under the SOA, the PCAOB is required to establish auditing and other related professional practice standards to be used by registered public accounting firms in the preparation and issuance of audit reports on public companies. All standards adopted by the PCAOB

must also be approved by the SEC. At the commencement of its operations, the PCAOB preserved the *status quo* by adopting on an interim basis existing standards, in each case as in existence on April 16,
2003:

- *Auditing*—the generally accepted auditing standards previously
promulgated by the American Institute of Certified Public Accountants and its Auditing Standards Board;

- *Attestation*—the Statements on Standards for Attestation Engagements and related interpretations and Statements of Position adopted by the AICPA Auditing Standards Board;

- *Quality Control*—the Statements on Quality Control Standards
adopted by the AICPA Auditing Standards Board and some
membership requirements of the AICPA's SEC Practice Section;

- *Ethics*—the provisions of the AICPA's Code of Professional
Conduct on integrity and objectivity, and related interpretations and rulings; and

- *Independence*—the provisions of the AICPA's Code of Professional Conduct on independence and some related standards
and interpretations of the former Independence Standards
Board.

These interim standards will remain in effect unless modified or replaced by the PCAOB or the SEC.

Under an auditing standard adopted in 2004, the PCAOB requires
registered public accounting firms to refer to "the standards of the
Public Company Accounting Oversight Board (United States)" in
their audit reports issued or re-issued on or after May 24, 2004, rather
than to U.S. generally accepted auditing standards, as was the case
previously. In addition, the PCAOB has adopted an auditing standard
governing the audit of internal control over financial reporting, discussed in chapter 3, and an auditing standard on audit documentation. It is expected to adopt other auditing and related professional
practice standards in the future.

Inspections of Registered Public Accounting Firms

Under the SOA, the PCAOB is required to conduct continuing inspections of registered public accounting firms. These inspections must occur annually with respect to firms having over 100 public company audit clients and at least once every three years for firms having 100 or fewer public company audit clients.

The PCAOB inspections will generally cover:

- inspection and review of selected audit and review engagements;

- evaluation of the sufficiency of quality control system; and

- testing of audit, supervisory and quality control procedures.

The PCAOB will issue a report in connection with each inspection.

Investigations and Disciplinary Proceedings

Under the SOA, the PCAOB has broad authority to conduct investigations of registered public accounting firms and their partners and employees and to impose disciplinary sanctions on them, including:

- temporary suspension or permanent revocation of a firm's registration;

- temporary or permanent suspension or bar of a person from further association with a firm;

- temporary or permanent limitation on the activities, functions or operations of a firm or its associated persons;

- civil money penalty for each violation;

- censure; and

- mandatory additional professional education or training.

All disciplinary sanctions are subject to SEC review.

Non-U.S. Public Accounting Firms

The SOA generally subjects non-U.S. public accounting firms that prepare or furnish audit reports with respect to a public company to the same requirements that apply to their U.S. counterparts. The PCAOB has issued some guidance relating to the oversight of non-U.S. public accounting firms. The PCAOB indicated that it will coordinate with non-U.S. regulatory authorities regarding the nature and scope of its oversight over non-U.S. firms so as not to subject non-U.S. firms to unnecessary burdens or conflicting requirements.

Organization and SEC Oversight of PCAOB

The PCAOB, established by the SOA on July 30, 2002, consists of five board members. Board members are appointed by the SEC, after consultation with the Federal Reserve Board and the Treasury Department, and serve on a full-time basis for staggered five-year terms. The PCAOB has its principal office in Washington, D.C. and regional offices in New York City, Atlanta, Dallas, San Francisco, Costa Mesa, Denver and Chicago.

Generally, no PCAOB standards or rules may become effective unless approved by the SEC. The SEC has the authority to review final disciplinary sanctions imposed by the PCAOB on registered public accounting firms or their associated persons and may also impose sanctions on the PCAOB itself.

Funding of PCAOB and FASB

To safeguard the independence of the PCAOB and the independence of the Financial Accounting Standards Board (FASB), which is a separate private-sector body responsible for establishing accounting standards, the SOA establishes a mandatory funding mechanism for both entities. The operations of both entities are funded through annual fees assessed on public companies, generally based on their relative market capitalization. Under the rules of the PCAOB, accounting firms are generally prohibited from issuing "clean" audit reports for any public company that has not paid both its PCAOB fees and its FASB fees. Companies that have paid their fees for the current year are listed on the PCAOB website.

References

Sarbanes-Oxley Act

§§ 101–09

SEC & PCAOB Websites (rules and commentary)

www.sec.gov/rules/pcaob.shtml

www.pcaobus.org/Rules_of_the_Board/index.asp

Chapter 13

Attorney Professional Responsibility

Overview

SEC rules expressly provide that an attorney representing a public company owes his or her professional and ethical duties to the company as an organization, as distinct from its officers, directors and employees. Relying on this guiding principle, which is drawn from pre-existing attorney professional standards, the rules require outside and in-house supervisory attorneys to report to the company's chief legal officer evidence of a "material violation" of certain U.S. securities and corporation-related laws.

An attorney must report further up the ladder to the company's audit committee or other committee, or to the full board of directors, if he or she does not, in the attorney's reasonable belief, receive an appropriate response from the chief legal officer.

The rules can be organized into three key conceptual elements, which are described in this chapter:

- covered attorneys;

- the trigger for reporting; and

- the procedure for reporting.

The rules were adopted by the SEC in 2003 to implement requirements of the Sarbanes-Oxley Act.

Covered Attorneys

In large measure, the scope of the rules is limited to U.S. attorneys directly handling SEC matters for public companies—in other words, SEC-reporting companies and companies with an initial registration statement on file with the SEC.

There is an explicit exemption for attorneys licensed outside the United States who (1) provide advice on compliance with U.S. securities laws only "incidentally to, and in the ordinary course of, the practice of law . . . outside the United States," or (2) provide advice on compliance with U.S. securities laws (or otherwise "appear and practice before" the SEC) "only in consultation with" U.S. counsel. The rules, however, extend to non-U.S. attorneys who practice outside the parameters of this exemption (as well as U.S. attorneys) who:

- advise that information need not be filed with the SEC, such as attorneys advising in connection with offshore Regulation S offerings and U.S. private placements; or

- provide advice regarding a document with notice that the document will be included or incorporated into SEC-filed materials, to the extent their advice relates to U.S. securities laws and regulations.

There is a degree of uncertainty whether an attorney engaged by a public company for an assignment that does not directly relate to the U.S. securities laws will be covered by the rules, since incidental questions relating to the securities laws may arise after the engagement has commenced or the company may determine to file a document with the SEC that was not originally expected to be filed.

The rule does not extend to an attorney who is only representing an unaffiliated third party (such as underwriters' counsel) in a transaction with the public company.

Reporting Trigger

The reporting trigger is the same for all covered attorneys, whether they work inside the company or for an outside law firm. Reporting is required when the attorney, while acting in the representation of a public company, either directly or indirectly through representation of a controlled person, becomes aware of "evidence" that a "material violation" has occurred, is ongoing or is about to occur on the part of the company or one of its directors, officers, employees or agents.

The SEC has adopted a complex standard for what constitutes sufficient evidence to require reporting. There must be "credible" evidence such that it would be "unreasonable, under the circumstances, for a prudent and competent attorney not to conclude" that the occurrence of the violation would be "reasonably likely."

In effect, the reporting trigger asks what a prudent and competent attorney under the circumstances would think about the evidence of which the potentially reporting attorney is aware. If some of those hypothetical attorneys could reasonably conclude no material violation was likely to have occurred (or be ongoing or about to occur), then the attorney is not obligated to report. If the only conclusion all the hypothetical reasonable attorneys would reach is the existence of a violation, the reporting obligation is triggered.

"Material violation" includes a material violation of U.S. federal or state securities laws or a material breach of U.S. federal or state common law or statutory fiduciary duty, including malfeasance, nonfeasance, abdication of duty, abuse of trust and approval of unlawful transactions. A material violation also includes a "similar material violation of any United States federal or state law." The reach of the term into "similar" material violations was driven by a phrase taken from the SOA section that required the SEC to issue the attorney professional responsibility rules, but the term is not defined in the SOA or the SEC rules.

Materiality is also left undefined by the rules. The SEC commentary accompanying the rules states that the term should be read as understood under the U.S. federal securities laws, citing leading cases that hold that information is "material" if, in the view of a reasonable investor, it would significantly alter the total mix of available information.

Reporting Procedures

The reporting obligations of an attorney under the rules depend on whether the attorney is subordinate or supervisory, whether the public company has a qualified legal compliance committee of non-employee directors and whether the attorney is in-house or outside counsel. An attorney under the supervision of another attorney, such as a law firm associate or a junior member of a corporate legal department, is required to report the evidence of material violation only to his or her supervisory attorney.

An attorney that is both a subordinate attorney and a supervisory attorney—in other words, an attorney who is in the middle of the seniority chain—may follow the rules for subordinate attorneys and need only report to his or her supervisory attorney evidence of a material violation of which he or she becomes aware, whether directly or through a report from a subordinate attorney, *unless* the mid-level attorney reports directly to the chief legal officer. In that case, he or she must follow the rules for a supervisory attorney and consider the appropriateness of the response and make any required further up-the-ladder reports.

A supervisory attorney is required to report evidence of a material violation of which he or she becomes aware, whether directly or through a report from a subordinate attorney. Any required report to the public company must be made first to the company's chief legal officer, unless the reporting attorney believes that such an approach would be futile. A report required to be made to the chief legal officer may also be made both to him or her and to the chief executive officer. A somewhat different reporting procedure, described below, applies if the company has a qualified legal compliance committee, which is relatively rare.

Obligations of Chief Legal Officer

When the chief legal officer receives a report, he or she must conduct whatever inquiry he or she reasonably believes is appropriate to determine whether the material violation described in the report has occurred, is ongoing or is about to occur. If the chief legal officer concludes there is no material violation, he or she must so advise the reporting attorney.

Unless the chief legal officer concludes there is not a material violation, he or she must take all reasonable steps to cause the company to adopt remedial measures to stop or prevent an ongoing or future violation and to rectify and minimize the possibility of recurrence of a past violation.

Further Reporting

Upon receiving the response from the chief legal officer, the reporting attorney must evaluate it. The reporting attorney must escalate and report to the audit committee unless the reporting attorney reasonably believes, based on the response from the chief legal officer, that there is no material violation. The reporting attorney also need not escalate if he or she reasonably believes that the company has adopted remedial measures or sanctions to stop or prevent an ongoing or future violation or rectify and minimize the possibility of recurrence of a past violation. The reporting attorney must also take these steps if the chief legal officer does not respond within a reasonable time. If the company has no audit committee, the report must go to another board committee composed entirely of non-employee directors or to the entire board.

Qualified Legal Compliance Committee

The rules permit reporting attorneys to follow a simpler procedure if the company has chosen to establish or designate a qualified legal compliance committee. In that case, the reporting attorney is not required to evaluate the response after making a report. Most public companies have chosen a wait-and-see approach and have not established such a committee.

A qualified legal compliance committee must consist of at least three non-employee directors, including an audit committee member. A qualified legal compliance committee would have the responsibility for investigating reports, notifying the audit committee or full board of directors, recommending remedial measures and sanctions to stop ongoing violations and rectify past violations and informing the chief legal officer, chief executive officer and board of the results of the investigations and measures to be adopted. The qualified legal compliance committee must have the authority to inform the SEC in the event the company does not implement the committee's recommendations in response to a report of a material violation.

If the public company has a qualified legal compliance committee, the reporting attorney has the option of reporting evidence of a material violation to the qualified legal compliance committee instead of the chief legal officer. If this alternative procedure is followed, the reporting attorney need not determine whether the response to a given report is appropriate. A qualified legal compliance committee could retain counsel to investigate material violation reports or to defend the issuer in a proceeding relating to any such report, and counsel for the committee would have no reporting obligations beyond the committee.

Reporting Obligations of Investigatory and Defense Counsel

The rules permit a limited exception from the attorney reporting requirements for attorneys retained or directed to investigate particular evidence of material violations or to defend the company in a proceeding relating to that evidence of a material violation. Investigatory counsel is exempted from up-the-ladder reporting beyond reporting to the chief legal officer, as long as the chief legal officer makes a report of any material violation found to the company's full board, appropriate committee or qualified legal compliance committee.

Defense counsel need not report evidence of a material violation up-the-ladder where the counsel has been retained or directed by the company's chief legal officer to "assert, consistent with his or her professional obligations, a colorable defense" relating to the evidence, and the chief legal officer regularly updates the company's board of directors, appropriate committee or qualified legal compliance committee as to the progress and outcome of the proceeding.

Permissive Reporting Beyond the Public Company

The rules permit, but do not require, an attorney appearing and practicing before the SEC in the representation of a public company to reveal to the SEC, without the consent of the company, confidential information related to the representation. Such a disclosure may be made to the extent the attorney reasonably believes is necessary to prevent the company from committing a material violation likely to cause substantial financial injury to the company or investors or from committing or suborning perjury or perpetrating a fraud on the SEC. Disclosure is also permitted if the attorney reasonably believes it necessary to rectify the consequences of a material violation that caused or may cause substantial financial injury to the company or investors if the attorney's services were used to further the violation.

Noisy Withdrawal Proposals

The rules as initially proposed in November 2002 contained "noisy withdrawal" provisions that would require an attorney who has not received an appropriate response within a reasonable time to his or her report of evidence of a material violation to submit written notices to the SEC. In this circumstance, the reporting attorney would be required to withdraw from the representation, so inform the SEC and disaffirm documents on file with the SEC that are tainted by the violation. A company's adoption of a qualified legal compliance committee would eliminate attorney withdrawal and SEC reporting obligations. The SEC implemented rules that do not currently contain noisy withdrawal provisions. However, the SEC stated that it would continue to consider the advisability of imposing such a requirement.

As of this writing, "noisy withdrawal" has not been imposed, and the SEC has not stated when or whether that may occur.

References

Sarbanes-Oxley Act

§ 307

SEC Rules

17 C.F.R. Part 205

SEC Website (rules and commentary)

www.sec.gov/rules/final/33-8185.htm

COMPLIANCE CHECKLIST:
Attorney Up-the-Ladder Reporting

Reporting trigger

Evidence of violation of US law by public company—direct observation or via report from another person

Lawyer has attorney-client relationship with the public company

Lawyer is practicing before the SEC

Violation relates to US or state securities law, to duties of directors, officers or employees under corporate law or to "similar" law

Only reasonable conclusion is that violation exists and is material

Reporting procedure

Subordinate attorney—operates under supervision of another attorney
> Report to supervising attorney
> No further action

Mid-level attorney—supervises others but is in turn supervised by a more senior attorney
> Report as for subordinate attorney
> *Except* attorney directly supervised by Chief Legal Officer must follow procedure for supervisory attorney—for example, Deputy General Counsel

Supervisory attorney—such as law firm partners and internal attorneys reporting directly to CLO
> Report to CLO
> Evaluate response for appropriateness
> If response not appropriate, report to Audit Committee
> Evaluate AC response for appropriateness
> If response not appropriate, so advise AC

Chief Legal Officer

> Receive report from other attorney *or* directly observe violation
>
> Investigate
>
> Respond appropriately (and promptly)
>
> Advise reporting attorney of response

Appropriate responses

Violation is not in fact a violation

Violation is not material

Violation has been stopped ⎫
                                      ⎬ and remedial action is being taken
Violation is no longer occurring ⎭

Issuer has retained investigating attorney and has implemented remedial recommendations or attorney has advised issuer has a colorable defense

Chapter 14

Employee Whistleblower Protection

Overview
Procedure
Remedies
Related Criminal Whistleblower Provision
Considerations for All Affected Employers
References

Overview

The Sarbanes-Oxley Act gives new legal rights to employees of public companies who claim they were retaliated against for providing information, assisting an investigation or participating in a proceeding concerning alleged violations of U.S. federal securities or anti-fraud laws.

In light of past experience with state whistleblower statutes, some representatives of management may be legitimately concerned that a provision such as this could be misused, for example, by individuals who know that their employment is about to be terminated and who might concoct allegations of "fraud." The statute does contain provisions to prevent misuse of its provisions, including requirements that claims must be brought within ninety days and that they be filed with the U.S. Department of Labor with only limited recourse to the

153

courts. The extent to which these provisions will be effective in discouraging manipulation of the statute is not yet known.

Procedure

An employee seeking relief under the statute must file a complaint with the U.S. Department of Labor within ninety days of the alleged violation. If the Department issues a decision on the complaint within 180 days, the decision will be final, subject only to appeal to the U.S. Courts of Appeals.

The employee filing the complaint bears the initial burden of establishing a case that the whistleblowing behavior was a "contributing factor" to the adverse employment decision. The employer may avoid a Department investigation by demonstrating, "by clear and convincing evidence," that it would have taken the same adverse employment action in the absence of the whistleblowing behavior.

Remedies

Remedies for violation of the statute include "all relief necessary to make the employee whole," including reinstatement, back pay and special damages such as attorney fees, litigation costs and expert witness fees. Punitive damages are not available.

One federal court has ruled that SOA whistleblower claims may be made subject to mandatory arbitration by an employment agreement.

Related Criminal Whistleblower Provision

It bears noting that the SOA also contains a related but generally more limited criminal provision. This part of the SOA specifies criminal sanctions consisting of fines or imprisonment up to ten years against anyone who, with the intent to retaliate, takes "any action harmful to any person, including interference with the lawful employment or livelihood of any person, for providing to a law enforcement officer any truthful information relating to the commission or possible commission of any Federal offense. . . ."

Although this criminal provision applies to a more limited scope of actions than the general whistleblower protection provision previously described, it applies to all persons and entities, including private companies.

Considerations for All Affected Employers

Among personnel practices that may merit review in light of the whistleblower provision are company procedures for internal complaints by employees, as well as the extent to which supervisors are instructed to respond appropriately to issues raised by subordinates.

For example, employers may want to review their policies regarding complaints of harassment and other co-worker misconduct and consider revising them to confirm explicitly that complaints or concerns about matters addressed in the SOA will be treated similarly.

As discussed in chapter 8, companies listed on the NYSE, Nasdaq or another U.S. stock exchange must also set up procedures for the "receipt, retention and treatment" of complaints regarding accounting, internal controls or auditing matters, and for the confidential, anonymous submission by employees of concerns regarding "questionable" accounting or auditing matters.

References

Sarbanes-Oxley Act
§§ 806 & 1107

Labor Department Rules
29 C.F.R. Part 1980

Labor Department Website
www.oalj.dol.gov/public/wblower/refrnc/68_31859.pdf
www.oalj.dol.gov/public/wblower/refrnc/sox1list.htm

Chapter 15

Investment Bank Research Analysts

Overview

The Sarbanes-Oxley Act required the SEC, either directly or acting through the NASD and the NYSE, to address conflicts of interest involving research analysts. The rules establish safeguards to separate research analysts from review, pressure or oversight from investment banking personnel and to limit company influence.

Some of the rules were in fact already in place, and some rules have been added. In addition, the SEC and other regulators reached a settlement in 2003 with ten leading U.S. investment firms regarding alleged conflicts of interest between equity research and investment banking. The firms agreed to adopt additional restrictions to separate research from investment banking. Many other investment firms have voluntarily adopted these restrictions as well.

NASD and NYSE Rules

The NASD and the NYSE implemented the SOA mandate through rules governing research analyst conflicts of interest that were adopted in several stages, primarily during 2002 and 2003, with some rules predating the SOA. The NASD regulates all U.S. broker-dealers, and the NYSE also regulates NYSE member firms, which include the major broker-dealers. Their rules in the research analyst area are essentially the same. These NASD and NYSE rules apply only to equity research and address the following major topics.

Research Department Separation

Under the NASD and NYSE rules, the research departments of NASD and NYSE member firms are insulated through restrictions on their communications, relationships and activities with non-research personnel of the firm and with companies that are the subject of research reports. Investment banking personnel and the broker-dealer firm generally are also expressly prohibited from threatening to retaliate against research personnel for unfavorable research that may adversely affect an investment banking relationship of the broker-dealer firm.

Prohibition on Research Soliciting Investment Banking Business

Research analysts are prohibited from participating in "pitch" meetings and other efforts to solicit investment banking business.

Analyst Compensation

Broker-dealer firms must establish a compensation committee to review and approve each analyst's compensation annually. The committee may not consider an analyst's contribution to the firm's investment banking business. Member firms also must annually certify to the NASD or the NYSE that each analyst's compensation has been documented, reviewed and approved.

Blackout on Research and Public Appearances in Connection with Offerings

Broker-dealers that manage or co-manage public securities offerings or that agree to participate as an underwriter or dealer in an offering, are prohibited from publishing research reports on the companies for a blackout period during and after the offerings. Public appearances by analysts during the same period are also prohibited.

The blackout for equity initial public offerings extends until forty days after the offering for lead and co-managers and until twenty-five days after the offering for other underwriters and dealers. For other equity offerings, the blackout period for all participating firms is ten days.

Research Blackout When "Lock-Ups" Expire

A manager or co-manager of a securities offering may not issue equity research within fifteen days before or after the end of any "lock-up" period relating to the offering.

Termination of Coverage

A broker-dealer firm that terminates research coverage of a company must provide notice of the termination and a final report that includes the firm's final recommendation or rating, unless it would be impractical.

Analyst Trading Restrictions

Research analysts may not trade against their own recommendations. The rules also impose quiet periods during which analysts may not trade securities issued by companies they follow and prohibit analysts from receiving securities of some companies prior to the initial public offerings.

Disclosure Requirement

Several disclosures must be made by broker-dealer firms that publish research, including disclosures regarding conflicts of interest, client relationships, compensation received from, and ownership of, companies that are the subject of research, definitions of ratings and historical rating and price target changes.

Analyst Exams

The rules establish registration, qualification and continuing education requirements for research analysts.

Supervisory Procedures

Broker-dealers must adopt written supervisory procedures to ensure compliance with the research analyst rules. A senior official of each member must annually attest that the firm has adopted and implemented the procedures.

SEC's Analyst Certification Rules

In addition to the NASD and NYSE rules described above, the SEC requires that analysts publishing research reports in the United States certify that the views expressed in the report accurately reflect the analyst's personal views about the subject securities and companies. The report must also disclose whether or not the analyst's compensation is directly or indirectly related to the specific views or recommendations expressed in the report.

This SEC certification applies to both equity and debt research, whereas the NASD and NYSE rules described above apply only to equity research.

Global Research Analyst Settlement

In addition, in 2003, the SEC, along with the NASD, the NYSE, the New York State Attorney General and other state securities regulators, reached a settlement of enforcement actions with ten leading investment firms in the United States regarding allegations of conflicts of interest between equity research and investment banking. The settlement imposed significant restrictions on equity research practices of the settling firms beyond those imposed on all U.S. broker-dealers by the rules previously discussed. The settlement restrictions are generally expected to apply until 2009. Following the settlement, many other U.S. broker-dealers also voluntarily adopted these restrictions.

The settlement addresses the following major topics:

- physical separation, separate reporting lines and communications firewalls between research and investment banking;

- stricter prohibition on research personnel soliciting investment banking business;

- prohibition on research personnel participating in "road shows" with respect to a securities offering or other investment banking transaction;

- banning investment bankers from directing marketing and selling efforts by research personnel;

- excluding investment bankers from research coverage decisions;

- issuance of a final report upon termination of research coverage;

- strengthened research oversight;

- removal of investment bankers from decisions about the research budget and compensation and evaluations of research personnel;

- dedicated legal and compliance staff for research;

- policies and procedures to prevent influence of research by non-research personnel;

- retention of a third-party independent monitor to review compliance with the settlement and report to the regulators; and

- additional conflict of interest disclosure requirements.

In addition, each of the ten settling firms must distribute without charge to its customers research from at least three different independent third-party firms to the extent those firms cover stocks covered by the settling firm. An independent consultant selects the third-party research firm.

References

Sarbanes-Oxley Act

§ 501

SEC Rules

Reg. AC

SEC Website (rules and commentary)

www.sec.gov/rules/sro/34-45908.htm

www.sec.gov/rules/sro/34-48252.htm

www.sec.gov/rules/final/33-8193.htm

www.sec.gov/spotlight/globalsettlement.htm

Chapter 16

Record Keeping

Document Preservation—Obstruction of Justice

There are two obstruction of justice provisions of the Sarbanes-Oxley Act that criminalize the destruction or alteration of documents with the intent to obstruct a government proceeding. Both provisions borrow heavily from pre-existing federal obstruction of justice laws and apply to any person, regardless of the person's or entity's status as a public company or as having a specified relationship with a public company. The provisions expand the reach of the law somewhat and increase penalties substantially, while not altering the substantive law.

Neither of the SOA provisions should reach genuinely routine document destruction. Thus, for example, the routine destruction of drafts of a quarterly earnings press release, Form 10-Q, 10-K, proxy statement or opinion of counsel would not violate the law in the absence of reason to believe that there is or will be a government investigation or proceeding, because it is done with the intent to discard the useless, not with the intent of "obstructing" an investigation or "impairing" availability for use in a proceeding.

In the current environment, however, the destruction of documents relating to, for example, a restatement of earnings due to accounting errors might raise issues, because it could be argued that one could reasonably foresee that such a restatement of earnings would trigger a government investigation.

Of course, once a company learns that a government investigation is likely or has been commenced (including a voluntary request for documents from the SEC), all relevant documents then existing, including emails and drafts, must be preserved. This may also include investigations of other parties where the conduct relates to the company.

Even if no investigation is existing or thought likely, the destruction of a record or document—including any drafts—for the specific purpose of making it unavailable in an investigation—actual, imminent or remote—would be imprudent and may well violate the law.

Retention of Audit Work Papers

U.S. and non-U.S. audit firms must retain for seven years most records relevant to their audits and reviews of financial statements of public companies. These records include work papers and other records (including electronic records) that contain conclusions, opinions, analyses or financial data related to the audit or review. The rule requires audit firms to retain documents that contain information or data that is "inconsistent" with the conclusions reached by the audit firm, as well as those that support the conclusions.

References

Sarbanes-Oxley Act
§§ 802(a) & 1102

SEC Rules
Reg. S-X Rule 2-06

Chapter 17

Remedies and Penalties

Officer and Director Bars

The Sarbanes-Oxley Act gives the SEC power to prohibit individuals from serving as directors or officers of public companies if they violate securities law antifraud provisions, such as Rule 10b-5 under the Exchange Act.

Under prior law, the SEC was authorized to seek to have an individual disqualified from serving as a public company director or officer, but only through obtaining a court order.

Civil Liability

Extended Statute of Limitations for Securities Fraud

The SOA lengthened the statute of limitations for private securities fraud actions to the earlier of five years after the alleged violation or two years after its discovery. Under previous law, the limitation was three years after the alleged violation and within one year of its discovery. The SOA is believed not to have changed the statute of limitations for bringing claims under the special federal prospectus and registration statement liability provisions applicable to securities offerings.

Nondischargeable Debts for Securities Fraud

The SOA amended the federal bankruptcy code to prevent the discharge of debts of individuals resulting from judgments, orders or settlements relating to the violation of federal or state securities laws or securities fraud or manipulation.

Establishment of Disgorgement Fund

The SOA empowers the SEC to establish a disgorgement fund using the proceeds of civil monetary penalties and settlements in enforcement actions for securities law violations for the benefit of victims of those violations. Previously those amounts were required to be turned over to the U.S. Treasury.

The SEC made its first major use of this FAIR Fund provision in May 2003 in a settlement against WorldCom, Inc. for its accounting fraud.

Criminal Penalties

Apart from the criminal provisions regarding document preservation, discussed in chapter 16, the SOA included several other enhancements to federal "white collar" and other criminal statutes, including increased potential monetary fines and prison terms and revisions to sentencing guidelines to indicate significantly longer prison sentences for white collar crimes that cause financial harm to large numbers of shareholders.

References

Sarbanes-Oxley Act

§ 308 and Titles VIII, IX and XI

United States Sentencing Commission Website

www.ussc.gov/guidelin.htm

Index

A

B

C

D

E

F

G

I

N

required disclosures, 53
Non-U.S. companies
as issuers covered by Sarbanes-Oxley Act, 3
non-GAAP financial measures, limited exceptions for disclosure
of use of, 57–58
Non-U.S. public accounting firms
Public Company Accounting Oversight Board (PCAOB)
requirements, 141
NYSE, *See* New York Stock Exchange (NYSE)

O

Obstruction of justice provisions
record retention, 163–64
Off-balance-sheet transactions
creation of obligation under, Form 8-K requirements for real-
time disclosures of, 64
Enron Corporation, 5–6
management's discussion and analysis (MD&A) disclosure of,
46–47
real-time disclosures, requirements under Form 8-K for
creation of obligation under off-balance-sheet arrangement, 64
triggering event accelerating or increasing obligation under
off-balance-sheet arrangement, 65
triggering event accelerating or increasing obligation under
creation of obligation under, Form 8-K requirements for
real-time disclosures of, 65
Officers, *See* Executive officers and directors
Outside auditors, *See* Auditors

P

S

T

U

W

X